How to Reach the Lost Generation

Brian Thomson

Destiny Image Publishers
P.O. Box 310
Shippensburg, PA 17257

"Speaking to the Purposes of God for this Generation
and for the Generations to Come"

ISBN 1-56043-132-6

For Worldwide Distribution
Printed in the U.S.A.

Thanks and Appreciation

I would like to thank God for blessing me with my wonderful wife, Connie, and four great kids: Joy, Ryan, Karissa, and Brayden.

I also greatly appreciate my senior pastors, Mel and Heather Mullen, for being such inspirational leaders and trainers for the past 15 years of my life.

I'd like to give special recognition to my wife, Connie, and two volunteers, Monica Prescott and Barb Brysh, for the many hours they contributed in helping type and edit the manuscript.

I thank Winkie Pratney, one of my greatest heroes, for writing the Foreword. His friendship, life style, books, tapes, and sermons have influenced me like those of none other. His practical help and vision for reaching today's generation of youth is unequalled!

Destiny Image books are available through these fine distributors outside the United States:

Christian Growth, Inc.
Jalan Kilang-Timor, Singapore 0315

Successful Christian Living
Capetown, Rep. of South Africa

Lifestream
Nottingham, England

Vision Resources
Ponsonby, Auckland, New Zealand

Rhema Ministries Trading
Randburg, South Africa

WA Buchanan Company
Geebung, Queensland, Australia

Salvation Book Centre
Petaling, Jaya, Malaysia

Word Alive
Niverville, Manitoba, Canada

Endorsements

"Brian Thomson is an outstanding pastor who understands the needs of today's youth. [This book] is a proven manual worked out in the crucible of the local church. The principles taught in this book will work in any local church where its leadership has a passion for youth."

Mel Mullen
Senior Pastor
Word of Life Centre
Red Deer, Alberta, Canada

"[This book] will stir you to action. The spirit of this book will 'rub off' on you. You will feel the author's heart as he speaks from his youth ministry experience.... Not only will you be 'taught,' you will be 'caught' by the fire-filled principles in this book."

Gregg Johnson
National Four Square Youth Director

"This practical manual for an explosive youth ministry combines personal testimony and teaching on how to develop a strong Christian youth group. Brian Thomson shares how a radical approach penetrated the blasé attitude among the youth group he leads and brought them into a 'reality encounter' with God."

Peter Youngren
Healing Evangelist

Table of Contents

Foreword

Introduction

Youth Ministry: Active Vision

Chapter 1	A New Breed	5
Chapter 2	No Spectators Allowed	17
Chapter 3	Training Champions	27
Chapter 4	Jehu: Zeal in Action	39
Chapter 5	Keys to Transformation	51

A Challenging Message

Chapter 6	The Challenge to Full Potential	69
Chapter 7	The Dating Challenge	83

Double Portion Anointing for Parents

Chapter 8	David and His Father	99
Chapter 9	Samson and His Parents	113

The Tower and the Battlefield

Chapter 10   The Tower: Action Youth Ministries 127

Chapter 11   The Battlefield: Zealous Exploits 141

Chapter 12   The Battlefield: Reaching Schools 155

Chapter 13   Supernatural Youth Ministry:
Uzziah, a Man of Action 167

Conclusion

Chapter 14   R.U.J. Who? 177

Foreword

How to Reach the Lost Generation

The edge of a great turning point in history, the time of the kings in the early records of the Bible was an epoch marked by corruption in high places, spiritual compromise, and violence in both the streets and the corridors of power, but also by genuine spiritual hunger.

One of God's "young guns" in that day was Jehu. He was known not only as a man very much on the move under the orders and purposes of God, but also as a prophetic voice of spiritual insight and conviction. The time has come again in history when we need to once more hear the voice of Jehu in the land, and in the faithfulness of God I see signs of His raising up young men and women who are doing just that. This book, written by my friend Brian Thomson, is a series of visions drawn from Jehu's life and times that will help you come to grips with some of the new directions in youth ministry that the Holy Spirit is developing in our day.

Brian Thomson represents part of the new breed of youth pastors and ministers who are caring, committed, and willing to push to the limit to see a generation of young people come to grips with their destiny in Christ.

You will find much in this book to challenge you and, if you obey it under God, much to change you. This book is a handbook for anyone with a passion for youth. I take pleasure in recommending both Brian's book and his ministry.

Winkie Pratney

Introduction

The greatest mission field still unreached in the world today lies right before our very eyes, and probably lives in our own homes. Greater than the Chinese population, greater than the vast and needy areas of the world, the greatest mission field is the young generation of today. More than half of the world's population is younger than 25, and we need to be trained how to reach this lost generation.

We need to understand their language and culture so we can present a credible gospel that relates to them. We must become more effective in not only reaching, but also training up a new generation of young people who will affect their world.

This book revolves around case studies from the biblical stories of such great heroes as Jehu, Elisha, David, Uzziah, and others. It has been prayerfully designed to equip youth leaders and parents alike with methods and suggestions to help them raise radical "youth of action" to their full potential in God.

I have had the joy of working with young people for 18 years. I am more convinced than ever that God has a plan for young people today. They have a definite part in God's plan even in the midst of their teen years. I believe that God will use this grouping of people more than any other in the next big revival in history.

For young people reading this book, I pray that you will be challenged by the Holy Ghost to become a greater force in the army that God is mustering together in this day, an army that will achieve great exploits! (See Isaiah 13:4.) This army, I believe, will be comprised of the greatest young people the world has ever seen. "A people come, great and strong, the like of whom has never been; nor will there ever be any such after them, even for many successive generations" (Joel 2:2b).

Youth Ministry:
Active Vision

And Elisha the prophet called one of the sons of the prophets, and said to him, "Get yourself ready, take this flask of oil in your hand, and go to Ramoth Gilead. Now when you arrive at that place, look there for Jehu the son of Jehoshaphat, the son of Nimshi, and go in and make him rise up from among his associates, and take him to an inner room. Then take the flask of oil, and pour it on his head, and say, 'Thus says the Lord: "I have anointed you king over Israel." ' Then open the door and flee, and do not delay." So the young man, the servant of the prophet, went to Ramoth Gilead. And when he arrived, there were the captains of the army sitting; and he said, "I have a message for you, Commander." Jehu said, "For which one of us?" And he said, "For you, Commander." Then he arose and went into the house. And he poured the oil on his head, and said to him, "Thus says the Lord God of Israel: 'I have anointed you king over the people of the Lord, over Israel. You shall strike down the house of Ahab your master, that I may avenge the blood of My servants the prophets, and the blood of all the servants of the Lord, at the hand of Jezebel.' " (2 Kings 9:1-7).

Then Jehu came out to the servants of his master, and one said to him, "Is all well? Why did this madman come to you?" And he said to them, "You know the man and his babble." And they said, "A lie! Tell us now." So he said, "Thus and thus he spoke to me, saying, 'Thus says the Lord: "I have anointed you king over Israel." ' " Then each man hastened to take his garment and put it under him on the top of the steps; and they blew trumpets, saying, "Jehu is king!" (2 Kings 9:11-13)

Chapter 1

A New Breed

A few years ago I was at the point of exhaustion. I had been battling with carnal teenagers who just wanted to have "fun" on Friday youth nights. "They don't want God or the Bible," I muttered, "just activities, games, and the opposite sex!"

I, however, wanted God to sweep in and kindle a revival in our youth group. I would stand up and say to this group, "God wants to move mightily on our lives and change us. I want you to believe with me for the moving of the Holy Ghost like we have never had." Their response was the one I dreaded: more criticism and complaint. The only way they could see the youth group get better was to fill up the schedule with wild activities, while their spiritual thirst would diminish.

One day, with great determination and boldness, I stood up and said, "We are not having any more sports nights or fun activities until we start seeking first the Kingdom of God. We will have prayer meetings, go evangelizing, and spend time listening to the Word of God with a fresh hunger." I was drawing the line. We were going to have a move of God or we were wasting our time.

For a while nothing really happened. Then the parents started complaining that their little Johnny wasn't enjoying youth meetings anymore. Most of my youth workers disagreed with the direction I was taking. I begged them to believe for a fresh stirring of the Lord in their lives and in our entire youth group and college and career group.

Then it happened. One day during chapel in our Christian school, I asked for those who were serious about serving God and who wanted to meet with God, to come up to the front. A short line of children and teenagers came and stood at the front.

As I began to pray for them, some of them started to fall down on the floor. Then more of them fell, until the entire group that came up were all lying on the floor. Everyone in the chapel service sat up and wondered what was happening.

Previously I had been critical when I saw things like that happen. I would say, "God can heal or touch people without their falling down." I thought people fell because the preacher "hyped" them up or pushed them down.

But this, I was convinced, was a move of God. Others came up for prayer. Students from every one of the 12 grades came up for prayer. The power of God was falling on almost everyone who asked for prayer. I remember little grade one students coming to the front and falling down, without anyone even touching them. It was absolutely beautiful to see the Lord touch them.

That night we had our youth meeting, and some teens testified of what God had done to them that day in the chapel service. Then I asked if any of the teens or singles would like to come forward for prayer. The same thing happened. God's Spirit started falling. Some people fell backwards so fast that no one had time to catch them. Others collapsed straight down so quickly that it was impossible to give them any assistance.

Many times these young people said they saw visions and heard the Lord talk to them as they were under the power of God on the floor. When one girl got up off the floor, there was a different look in her eyes. It was a look of fire and zeal. It was a look that said, "I met God and I will never be the same again!" Her look said, "I will live for God the rest of my life." She was changed from that moment on. She started witnessing, preaching, and winning souls.

That day we received a breakthrough. For months afterward, in every youth service and chapel service, the power of God would come down in similar ways.

At one chapel service, the power of God came in so suddenly that a group of students at the altar all went down together. I was amazed to count five layers of people in the pile. Legs were jumbled over legs and arms over arms—15 students in a pile. At every service, these students didn't just go down under the power and then get up again. Many of them laid there motionless for 15 minutes, others for 30 minutes and some for more than 2 hours.

In service after service God moved and touched young people's lives. At times the Holy Spirit spoke to us about sins in our lives. Such a strong sense of His presence caused us, one by one, to begin repenting. I remember one of the hard-hearted young men in the school. He was one of the real cool tough guys who was trying his hardest not to let God touch him, but in one of these meetings God got through to him. He came up to the front and started repenting before the entire school for the way he was living. With tears filling his eyes, he asked his schoolmates to forgive him. Then, one by one, all the other tough guys stated that they too were making a new dedication to live for God, and they repented for the life style they had been living. They confessed that they had been bad examples and asked for forgiveness from other students for the way they had treated them.

As you can imagine, chapel services were lasting quite a bit longer. Nothing can replace God's touching and softening hearts. Sometimes all the love and friendship we give to hard teens doesn't do a thing. We need a moving of the Holy Ghost.

Young people started to get saved in our youth meetings. Beforehand it had been so hard to get new people to come and even harder to lead them to receive Christ. Now young people were coming and getting saved. Groups of them would come in together. Many times these new teens didn't know what was happening. We would ask if we could pray for them. When we gathered around them to pray, the power of God would come on them and they would fall to the floor too. Some of these young people have now graduated from our Bible College and are on staff in our church or in one of our branch churches. Many others have become vital members who are still pillars in the church.

Not only were we meeting God and getting right with Him, but God also was sending His Holy Spirit to empower us to serve Him. We taught on receiving the baptism of the Holy Ghost, and those who had not already received the baptism with their prayer language of speaking in tongues came up and received.

God was doing so many things—every service for months was so powerful, and yet so different. Teenagers looked forward to every service. We never had to coax them to come. Without any persuasion from the staff they would sing, lift their hands in the air, and praise their Lord. I would see tears coming from their eyes and faces lighting up with a glow of God's presence.

I remember on another occasion in one of the school's chapel services that I felt the power of God come in as a cloud to my left. I started to say, "The power of God is moving over here...." As soon as I pointed to the section, a row of teenagers and children who were standing, collapsed and fell on the floor and on each other. One young girl in elementary school fell so fast and hard that she hit her head on the hard metal chair as she went down. It was the Lord, though, so no one ever got hurt.

When this girl got up, she started singing a beautiful song of the Lord. God was releasing the gifts of His Spirit on these young people that day. Then we started teaching on the gifts of the Spirit and many of the youth began prophesying and moving in the gifts of the Spirit.

A very shy girl had quietly slipped into the back row for weeks during this time. One service, as God was moving, I sent back a youth worker to ask if she would like us to pray for her. She said she would let us pray for her on one condition—that no one would lay hands on her. We promised. As soon as I started to pray, "Lord Jesus, bless this young lady..." she fell straight back, stiff as a board, and hit the floor. No one caught her. Like many others, she laid there for about an hour. This girl was completely changed by this experience. She was like Peter before and after the day of Pentecost—once shy but then bold as a lion and anointed by the Holy Ghost. She joined us in praying for others. When she touched someone, it was as if the anointing was still on her, flowing into the person we were praying for, and that person also would go under the power of God. God started to use her powerfully in words of knowledge and in the gift of prophecy.

God continued to pour out the gifts of the Spirit in a dynamic way in every meeting. It was exciting as we began to teach and encourage everyone to pray for each other and to believe for healing and miracles. God poured out His Holy Spirit and young people were seeing God work miracles. Often our hands would get hot as we prayed for people to get healed. Once I was praying for a young man about eight years old and my hand was getting hot. I felt this boy's head and his hair was hot! We invited a few other young people over to see what God was doing. They all felt the power of God on top of this young man's head. It was like the top of a stove that was so hot you could not even put your hand on it. Eventually, the whole chapel of 75 students came over, touched his hot hair, and gave glory to God.

During those months God launched our youth group in a whole new direction. An evangelism explosion began; then a Saturday training school evolved, which we called "Go-Team Training." We began to take music and drama teams of young people all over Western Canada and on mission trips overseas. Souls were getting saved and our youth group was growing and exciting. Many of our grade 12 students, college and career people, and new converts were demanding that we start some type of full-time training. That year we began a four-month summer "Go-Team Training," then that fall we started Word of Life Bible College.

The Bible says in Psalm 110:3, "Your people will offer themselves willingly in the day of Your power, in the beauty of holiness and in holy array out of the womb of the morning; to You [will spring forth] Your young men, who are as the dew" (AMP).

Getting a visitation of the Holy Ghost is the key! When God comes in power, your youth group will be changed. It will be like a fresh dew experience to you and your church. Young people will rise as the dew of the morning. What a joyful sight that is! They will be full of zeal and dedication.

They will offer themselves willingly to serve the Lord. One translation of Psalm 110:3 says that they will be "volunteers" in the day of His power (NKJ).

We must continually have a visitation of God that stirs our teenagers with a fresh desire to "want to" live for God, not "have to." When they have experienced God, they will "want" to be trained for evangelism and for doing exploits.

Equipped With a Powerful Anointing

This kind of visitation is what happened to Jehu in Second Kings 9. He was in the army just sitting around doing nothing. His army was losing. Then a young man sent by Elisha the prophet gave him a word from God, and the transforming power of God settled on Jehu. He came out of that experience a changed man. He started to charge forward with an unequaled zeal. That is what will happen to you and I as well as to young people today.

This story begins with God impressing on Elisha's heart to call for a young, unnamed prophet. Elisha was a mighty man of God who had a double anointing of the great prophet Elijah. Elisha can be compared to church leaders, senior pastors, youth workers, parents, and others who are instrumental in orchestrating a Holy Ghost plan to involve young people.

This powerful man of God selected a young prophet in training, and commissioned him to do a Holy Ghost job.

And Elisha the prophet called one of the sons of the prophets, and said to him, "Get yourself ready, take this flask of oil in your hand, and go to Ramoth Gilead" (2 Kings 9:1).

Elisha was interested in training up others. He wasn't preparing for retirement! He wanted to get others involved in the work of the Lord too! Maybe he remembered how Elijah had given him some small jobs to do and how it had helped him grow into a powerful ministry. So Elisha called a young man to assist him in what he was doing. He knew that he must lay foundations in younger men so they might carry on the next move of God.

We have great pastors, mighty men and woman of God who are the foundation and keys to the movings of God, but God wants them to invite the young people onto the battlefield and call them into action as well.

Some people have the mentality that a person must be older to be used by God. But we know that the Bible says *young men* will *see visions* and *sons and daughters will prophesy* (see Acts 2:17). We know all the stories in the Bible, which are written for our example, of young men like Josiah, who became king at eight years old (see 2 Kings 22:1). We know the great victory over the giant Goliath that David gained as a young man in his teens (see 1 Sam. 17). Why then are young people overlooked, forgotten, or left out until they mature?

Today there is a fresh call of God to go beyond the great stories of the Bible. God is looking to and fro, searching the earth to find willing, ready, and obedient people. He's choosing them and calling them, and as they respond and begin to seek Him and get to know Him, they will be strong and do exploits! (See Daniel 11:32.) What are exploits? According to Webster's 1828 dictionary, exploits are "heroic acts or deeds of renown; great or noble achievements." God has a high calling for everyone to do great things through the power of His Spirit.

Elisha was a man of God who knew the plan of God for his day. God spoke to Elisha to go anoint Jehu as the next king of Israel. Today the starting point of revival and awakening that turns a new generation to God is the point when God speaks to a man and gives him a plan, a strategy, the mind of God. You see, God's plan is never limited to just one age group of people. God raises up whomever He wants.

Youth workers need to hear what the Lord is saying for today. What is God's plan for reaching today's young generation? We cannot concentrate or base our plans on something that worked ten years ago; we must find the mind of God for today. We must seek God for our part in His plan. We have got to have a fresh word from God. When God speaks, He floods us with faith and creative energy to accomplish the task.

For whatever is born of God overcomes the world (1 John 5:4a).

Whatever is born of God or originates with God overcomes the world. We need ideas and strategies that are born of God to touch the teenagers in our churches, in our families, and in our land.

That reminds me of the story of Joshua in the Book of Joshua, chapters 1 through 6. You can imagine what went through Joshua's mind when he heard that Moses was dead and he was in charge. He himself now had to hear God and lead the nation of Israel into the Promised Land. Joshua had a lot of faith for taking the land when Moses was the leader, but now he was the leader, the one to hear God and perform the mighty miracles.

Joshua, as the new leader of the nation of Israel, had a big job to do in leading the army of Israel to the great walls of Jericho. Unbelief, fear, and doubt could have filled Joshua's heart. God, however, told him to be strong and very courageous. Later God gave him a revelation of how to win and how the walls would fall down.

God has specific direction available to overcome the great obstacles and challenges we face in youth ministry. God is looking for youth leaders who will seek God for His plan and who will have faith in that plan and move forward. We need to be people who will respond to His call in faith. God is looking for young people today who will hear the call and rise up with a risk-taking boldness that causes them to step out and do something great for God. It is thrilling to hear God's plans and instructions for reaching young people for Jesus.

I believe God is raising up young people all over the world. His hand is beginning to rest on certain ones who have responded with the heart attitude that He is looking for to execute His plan. God's sovereign hand is in control. He is setting the stage and molding the people, getting everything ready.

Just as Elisha called for the young, unnamed prophet, so is God calling for young people who may appear to be insignificant, and He's giving them a vision. He is giving them a reason for living. He is giving them a mandate to go forward for Him.

A call from the Lord is being heard in the land for young people to arise and play a vital part in His plan. The Church once had a mentality that young people didn't want to serve God, but people are realizing that isn't true. Young people want to be called from being just bored spectators, from sitting along the sidelines watching the good fight of faith, into the excitement and action of being on the front lines.

I believe that one thing that absolutely delights the heart of God is when a young person decides to really get passionate for God. They will get so on fire for God that they say "no" to the things of the world, the flesh, and the devil. All they can think about is loving God, winning the lost, and doing things that please Him. God is pleased when young people choose to do His will and when that choice comes from their hearts.

A New Breed

We need to be desperate for a move of God. Then a message from God will come to our spirits and show us what we are to say and do. This visitation of God will come to our children and young people! I believe Psalm 110 can happen to your youth group too! The transforming power that changed our youth and transformed Jehu into another man will be sent from God to your young people. The power of God is coming to *empower us*—to form a new breed of young workers. A new breed of radical young people is on the horizon. They will zealously live for God and do *great exploits*.

Chapter 2

No Spectators Allowed

Where there is no vision, the people perish (Proverbs 29:18a KJV).

I believe youth workers and parents can be like Elisha. He was someone who had a double portion of Elijah's anointing. Every youth worker needs to get on their knees and cry to God for the empowering of the Holy Ghost to affect this generation. "Lord, give me a double portion of Your Spirit!" Every parent needs an ability that goes beyond their human wisdom to raise their children in this day.

As parents of four wonderful children, my wife Connie and I depend more than ever on the leading and empowering of the Holy Ghost in raising our children to be dynamic and greatly used by the Lord. Two verses that I am claiming are Psalm 112:1-2. "Praise the Lord! Blessed is the man who fears the Lord, who delights greatly in His commandments. *His descendants will be mighty on earth....*" In a later chapter I will talk about two sets of parents who were instrumental in raising up powerful young men. I believe parents can be anointed by the Holy Ghost to raise up champions.

Elisha was someone who grasped hold of God's plan as a seer (or prophet). It's a fresh day for us to be see-ers of what the Lord's vision is today and then to have a clear understanding of what He has called us to do.

I like going to God in prayer by claiming Amos 3:7. "Surely the Lord God does nothing, unless He reveals His secret to His servants the prophets." I pray, "Lord, I know You want to do some great things in my life and in the lives of these young people! You say that You won't do anything without first showing Your prophets. Lord, open my eyes to see what You are wanting to do. Help me to not be in a rut in my ideas of how I think You should move. Give me vision, Lord, and fill me full of zeal."

...your enthusiasm has stirred most of them to action (2 Corinthians 9:2 NIV).

When I catch the vision of what God wants to do, I get motivated and a fire starts to burn in me. God doesn't want us to just maintain and survive in youth ministry; He wants us full of zeal as leaders and as parents. It is awesome to realize the weight of responsibility on all parents, youth pastors, and leaders. What a challenge it is! So we must first get fresh enthusiasm and vision from the Lord, then we can motivate our teenagers.

*...most of them have been fired by **your zeal*** (2 Corinthians 9:2 NEB).

Many times over the years, I have said to our young people, "The youth group you are a part of today will not stay the same. It is going to change and be different! We will become more dynamic and do greater things for the Lord! God will train up and anoint more and more of you and we will go forth...." Speak change. Speak vision into them continually! Get them excited about the possibilities in the Lord. Get their hopes up in the Lord. Keep them looking to the future with purpose, plans, vision, and anticipation, dreaming about how God will use them.

Elisha's Plan to Raise Up Jehu

Elisha, in this case study of the launching of Jehu's ministry, knew what God wanted to do and was very instrumental in bringing it to pass.

The story of Jehu is an exciting episode in the Bible, but I want to focus for a while on another part that I enjoy: the unnamed prophet and how he is used by the Lord.

And Elisha the prophet called one of the sons of the prophets, and said to him, "Get yourself ready, take this flask of oil in your hand, and go to Ramoth Gilead" (2 Kings 9:1).

Elisha chose this young prophet and told him to get himself ready for a mission. This young man responded to the invitation to be used by God. He prepared himself because he recognized the opportunity in the invitation issued by the great prophet to do an assignment.

I have found over and over again that when young people can grasp the idea that God wants to use them, they get excited. They become like the disciples, who left everything to follow Jesus. Young people need to be called and chosen to come alongside others in the ministry. They must be invited into practical service for the Lord, not just left to sit and learn. God can and wants to use them right now. You need to find places in the church where they can serve God.

God is not looking for superstars (although we all have superstar potential in God's eyes). He is looking for someone who wants God to show Himself mighty on his behalf (see 2 Chron. 16:9).

A vital part of God's plan is to use the young people with their zeal, enthusiasm, and dedication to do something that has "adventure" written all over it.

For too long the young people in church and their youth groups have just been baby-sat or entertained. God is calling young people to come out of their lives of idleness, out of the bleachers as spectators, and into the adventure of exploits. The main reason some youth groups encounter negativity is, *spectators turn into criticizers!*

It always amazes me how critical we can get when we sit and watch sports on TV or when we go to a sports event and sit in the crowd with thousands of fans. One minute everyone is clapping and cheering on the home team because they are doing so well, yet as soon as one of their heroes makes a mistake or the team loses the game, the once-adoring fans quickly turn into the team's worst criticizers. Suddenly they are blasting the team, the coach, and the players. If the fans are so brilliant and skilled at the sport, why aren't they the ones playing?

Young people are just like that. When they are limited to only watching, it is an inevitable fact that they will turn into criticizers. It won't matter how many laser lights you have, or how many pyrotechnic effects, or how much anointing is present. They will get negative, murmur, and criticize.

They need an invitation into action. A critical sports crowd would be silenced if they were given the ball and asked to do better than the professional athletes.

Young people don't want to sit around and watch. They want to have people believe in them and hand them the ball.

We need to tell our teenagers how valuable they are to us and to God! We need them on our team! We must make sure they know how significant they are. Most importantly, we need to motivate and challenge them to get involved and use their giftings and talents.

Teenagers are full of energy and life and if we don't win them over to serving God and channeling their energy into areas of ministry, they will do something else with their time that could be destructive.

A very interesting Scripture, Ezekiel 16:49-50, tells us what steps led to the destruction of Sodom and Gomorrah. How did they become so perverse? The Bible says that the iniquity of Sodom was her "pride, fullness of food, and *abundance of idleness;* neither did she strengthen the hand of the poor and needy" (v. 49). When young people are left without the challenge of serving God with their time, they will do whatever they feel like doing. That idleness of time will be sucked up by television, music, and friendship, all of which will become sour and negative. We can't sit back and watch this great potential turn to sin and perversion.

In the parable of the workers in the vineyard, in Matthew 20, Jesus told about the man who went into the city and found people standing idle and called them to work in the harvest. In this same manner we must find teenagers and challenge them to serve God. We must challenge them to come out of idleness and present their time as a living sacrifice to God.

Teenagers are active people. They need to be involved. The Bible teaches that each member, no matter what age, is "indispensable" (see 1 Cor. 12:22 NIV). Each has a vital part and is placed by the Holy Ghost in the Body with a job to do. He wants them to have a part, not just watch others do exploits.

God is calling young people from the idleness that could lead to perversion to meaningful, fulfilling involvement in the Lord's harvest. He is calling them from being simply spectators who become negative and scornful, to becoming people who make valuable contributions to His plan. God is calling them off the stands and challenging them to get into the game and play a key role in the next move of God.

An important aspect of the Body of Christ is that every member has a ministry. The pastor is not the only full-time minister in the congregation. Every member works full-time for God. The pastor's main job is not to do all the work of the ministry, but to train and equip others to do it! (See Ephesians 4:12.) An accurate test to evaluate the success of a five-fold minister is this: Are the saints doing the work of the ministry? If the saints are watching the pastor do all the ministry, then the pastor is not doing what God wants him to do. He must train and release the saints to do the work of the ministry.

Young people need leaders like Elisha in their church who will call for them and give them jobs to do. It is not the will of God for teenagers to sit around at popular hangouts in boredom, wondering what to do. It's a day for them to hear the call of God and to rise in response to the call and do something great for the Lord.

Don't Limit What the Lord Wants to Do Through Teens

Even television programs express the desire of the youth culture to do incredible feats. One recent television show was about a teenager who was a doctor. This indicates the cry of young people today to do something outstanding and above the limitations with which others have boxed them. Even Jesus, at age 12, confounded the teachers and the scribes (see Lk. 2:46-47).

> *Do not neglect the gift that is in you, which was given to you by prophecy.... . Meditate on these things; give your-self entirely to them, that your progress may be evident to all* (1 Timothy 4:14-15).

God will speak to your young people and bring a stirring to their spirits. Then they will separate themselves unto the Lord for His call on their lives. They will have fresh purpose to stay holy and pure, to get into the Bible and pray, and to help others.

I have written to you, young men, because you are strong, and the word of God abides in you, and you have overcome the wicked one (1 John 2:14b).

He who overcomes, I will make him a pillar in the temple of My God... (Revelation 3:12).

Young people need a determination to be overcomers. They need to overcome the things of this world and set their sights on higher things. Then God can transform them from spectators in the church to pillars who help usher in the next move of God.

Don't fall into the maintenance mode of youth ministry. Instead train them and watch as God calls them to do fantastic things.

For I will work a work in your days which you would not believe, though it were told you (Habakkuk 1:5b).

Man has always limited what God can do. The children of Israel in the wilderness did just that.

*How often they provoked Him in the wilderness, and grieved Him in the desert! Yes, again and again they tempted God, and **limited** the Holy One of Israel* (Psalm 78:40-41).

We know that God is a God of miracles, but when we look at the teenagers in our house or in our youth group, our vision can soon be limited.

We should not be like Samuel was when he looked with his natural eyes at who could be the next king of Israel. God looks at young people in a different manner then we do. In this situation Samuel looked on the exterior. He saw the older brothers of David and said, "Surely the Lord's anointed is before him!" God, however, looks on the heart (see 1 Sam. 16:6-7).

God is not looking for talented, muscular, or smart teenagers as much as He is for people with David's heart. He is looking for young people with an intense love for Him. He doesn't choose the high and mighty or the noble.

But God has chosen the foolish things of the world to put to shame the wise, and God has chosen the weak things of the world to put to shame the things which are mighty (1 Corinthians 1:27).

Maybe some of you are saying, "The young people I am involved with are dead and boring. I can't see any potential." You need to allow the Lord to change your mentality and to give you revelation. You need to let the Lord open the eyes of your understanding and be enlightened, that you may know what is the hope of His calling on their lives (see Eph. 1:18). God is a God of purpose and He has a great purpose and destiny for each one of them!

Youth workers can easily overlook the young people who are right in front of them. These workers are praying that God will send them some dynamic, quality teenagers, but most of the time these quality young people are sitting right before their eyes. Often youth workers can't see past the different hairstyles or mannerisms. So view your youth group or children's group as a gold mine, as diamonds in the rough. Know that God has set you in the right place, a place where you can be the one to influence them. The other side of the coin is true too, that God has sent them to you to help develop and train you in your ministry.

Jesus saw Peter in the natural realm as a pebble, but through the eye of faith and destiny He knew Peter was called to be a boulder for God. God sees us for what we can become. Look at young people prophetically. Covet the gift of prophecy. The things that God will show you as a parent or leader about your young people will astound you! As

God shows you these things, respond in faith and say, "I believe Your word, Lord. Now help me to train them up and to see them as You saw Peter."

Nothing is more exciting than when God moves in and touches people's lives. God can move by His Spirit and do a quick work in your young people's lives. Get rid of the mentality that says it will take months or years for God to do something dynamic in your youth group.

God can use you mightily to affect young people. Remember, you can be equipped with a double portion of God's Spirit to do what He has called you to do!

Chapter 3

Training Champions

Today's church teenagers are more hungry for the Bible than I have ever seen before. Some of them have had stories and games all their lives, and they are ready for deeper truths, wanting Bible studies. They are ready to be trained in "boot camp" for the real "war." Unsaved teenagers know very little about the Bible, but are very interested! I encourage you to look at your schedule and find a time for extra training. You might be surprised at who will come.

I believe that all Christians are called to be workers in the Kingdom of God. Ministry is not just for the ones who feel they will be on the staff of a church someday. Even though the young prophet used by God was in training to be a full-time prophet, he is still a model for us of how God wants to use everyone in our youth groups for Him, no matter what aspect of vocational work they will enter in the future. We are all full-time for Jesus.

As God works in your youth group, there will be young people who will respond joyfully to opportunities for serving God. You need to have a vision for training them and your key workers with you.

Now when you arrive at that place, look there for Jehu the son of Jehoshaphat, the son of Nimshi, and go in and make him rise up from among his associates, and take him to an inner room. Then take the flask of oil, and pour it on his head, and say, "Thus says the Lord: 'I have anointed you king over Israel.' " Then open the door and flee, and do not delay (2 Kings 9:2-3).

The young prophet needed special instructions on what to do. There is a tremendous need for specialized training to be a worker. Much of the training we do in our youth meetings, Bible College, and college and career group, is based on the training Jesus gave His 12 disciples.

Jesus Trained His Disciples

Matthew 10 and Luke 10 tell us of Jesus' training the 12 and the 70 disciples. Jesus gave them specific training in evangelism—where to go, what to say, and what to expect.

But when He saw the multitudes, He was moved with compassion for them... . Then He said to His disciples, "...Therefore pray the Lord of the harvest to send out laborers into His harvest" (Matthew 9:36-38).

Jesus saw the multitudes of people and the big task before Him, and He proceeded to solve the problem with more helpers. He called unto Him His disciples and started to teach and train them. It is essential that every youth ministry is actively training up workers, core teenagers and any other young people who will come for training.

Pray for More Workers

Now it came to pass in those days that He went out to the mountain to pray, and continued all night in prayer to God. And when it was day, He called His disciples to Himself; and from them He chose twelve whom He also named apostles (Luke 6:12-13).

Jesus chose the 12 apostles after praying all night long. For your key leaders, you need to seek God and select the disciples that God wants you to train. Pray like this, "God, which ones do you want me to choose?"

One day I was very disappointed with the workers I had helping me. They were dragging along with a deadness and apathy that was depressing to me. They had lost any real spark of life. I started to pray with desperation that God would fire up these workers and send more workers to help with the harvest that God was adding to our youth group. One answer to that prayer was a young girl named Marney. She had been coming to our church for about two weeks. I will never forget the night that she responded to an altar call. After receiving prayer, she fell under the power of God and remained motionless for more than two hours. When she stood up, she looked totally different! Her eyes were glowing and the anointing of God was all over her. It was like the Lord had moved on her sovereignly, rewired her, and changed her heart. From that time on Marney has never been the same. She grew in God so fast that she passed all the other youth workers. Today Marney is married and on our church staff.

Recruit Workers

I love the stories of how Jesus called His disciples. Some of them He walked up to and simply said, "Follow Me, and I will make you fishers of men" (Mt. 4:19). It seems that Jesus merely said, "Follow Me," and then just kept walking. There were some who noticed that this Man was someone special. He was One they would like to follow, so they dropped their nets and followed Him.

As you live zealously for God, many will admire you, want to follow you, and count it a privilege to spend time with you. Personally invite others to spend time with you and to do different ministry projects. Ask them to go evangelizing or to pray with you. Many will enjoy the privilege. It is not necessarily that you are anyone special, but God stirring their hearts.

Watch for the ones who are fervent for the Lord. Look for the ones whom God is touching by His Spirit. Ask them if they would like to help you in some aspect of youth ministry. As you begin to spend time with the disciples you are choosing to train, you will sense that some of them have a full-time call of God. It is important to start grooming them a little extra and stirring them to respond to the call of God that is on their lives.

Look for both adults and young adults who have a burden for teenagers in your church. One time I was praying and asking God for more workers to be involved in youth ministry. I was wanting to train up others in a team with me. Soon after that we were having a work bee to upgrade some of our property, and I noticed a certain young man helping us pull up trees. I had never seen him before in my life, yet God told me, as soon as our eyes met, that I was to start training him.

When he had completed the task he had been doing, I went over to him, introduced myself, and asked, "Have you ever considered being involved in youth ministry?" His face lit up and he told me his story. Years before he had been aflame for God and had felt a call to youth ministry. But with the pressures of dating he fell in love, took his eyes off God, and backslid. The young lady he fell in love with became pregnant and they were married.

A few years later, their youngest child died. He said that God used that death to turn him back to God. In fact, just a week before I met him, our pastor had performed the funeral and led him back to Christ.

When I came up to him and asked him if he had ever considered youth ministry, it was as if God was giving him another chance. He became extremely excited and started helping me with the younger teenagers. He had an excitement and a zeal that was incredible. He seemed to be making up for lost time. He and his wife became wonderful friends and co-workers with us as we served God together.

Teach and Train Workers

And seeing the multitudes, He went up on a mountain...and taught them... (Matthew 5:1-2).

Jesus spent a lot of time teaching His disciples. He spent time with them, instructing them, answering their questions, and adjusting their thinking and attitudes.

Often Jesus trained His disciples with a "learning and doing" style. After all, it takes more than classroom instruction to train. Jesus would first teach about healing the sick, then He would model how to do it. Then Jesus gave them power to heal the sick and let them do it while He watched. Jesus then sent them out on their own to do it. When they came back, He asked for a report and then evaluated their ministry and gave them further instruction.

One example of this training is seen in His sending out the 70 disciples in Luke 10. In verses 1-16 Jesus instructs them about where they should go and what they should say. Verse 17 says that the 70 returned with joy. Jesus rejoiced with them over the good report, but then gave them input to stay focused on the fact that their names were written in Heaven rather than on having demons in subjection to them (v. 20).

Young people want to learn and do. Think of ways to train them, not just to teach them. Invite them to assist you with some different projects they can help with and some jobs they can do to see souls get saved and the power of God flow through them. Try to give an application and involvement to everything you teach them to do.

In the process of training you will become good friends with your disciples. Often they will become some of your best friends. Jesus' best friends were His disciples and He loved them to the end (see Jn. 13:1).

It is a serious challenge from the Lord to train up a team of people. We have a responsibility to train the ones whom God brings our way, the ones whom He raises up and puts an anointing on.

Many young people today want to live for God, but they have problems that need healing and solving. Sometimes the best thing to do is meet with them privately and talk to them about their lives and what frustrations they have. Talk to them about the things God is saying to them. Ask them about their desires and dreams. Sow into them what you think God can do in their lives, and how exciting it is to serve God.

...take this flask of oil in your hand, and go... (2 Kings 9:1).

Elisha handed the anointing oil to the unnamed young man and told him to go. What a noteworthy verse that is! We need to get the anointing and then *go* for God. This is similar to the way God told Samuel to "fill your horn with oil" and "go" and anoint David as king of Israel in First Samuel 16:1. God doesn't send us out empty; He gives us the anointing to do the task.

When I was 16 years old and a brand-new Christian, I felt God calling me into full-time ministry. It was an exciting time in my life, but also one of the scariest. I hated reading books and the Bible was so big. I dreaded standing in front of the class at school, and standing in front of people is all preachers seemed to do. I didn't think I could do it.

In a time of insecurity about the call of God on my life, my ability, and what I could do for God, God burned this

Scripture into my heart and I have never forgotten it. It continues to help me to this day.

> *If anyone speaks, let him speak as the oracles of God. If anyone ministers, let him do it as with the ability which God supplies, that in all things God may be glorified through Jesus Christ, to whom belong the glory and the dominion forever and ever. Amen* (1 Peter 4:11).

God promised that He would help me, be with me, and give me the words to say, as well as a supernatural ability. Young people need to know that God will help them, that He will empower them! It is a great privilege to feel the Lord using you. What an honor it is to know that God is using the words you say and the things you do, for His glory.

How to Get Young People More Involved

1. You must have a training mentality. Once I spoke in a youth group whose youth pastor was doing everything. He was leading songs, doing the preaching, coming early to set up chairs and staying late to do the vacuuming. His work and attitude were heroic, but he was the only one getting the reward for serving God. It is vital to gather a team and give them opportunity. Move over and let them in. Instill into them the zeal and joy you have in serving God.

2. Teach the motivational giftings found in Romans 12:4-8. Make sure they know that they have talents from the Lord. Teach them how rewarding it is to be used by God. People need to know they are special and significant. God created them with a job to do for His Kingdom.

3. Get a plan in motion in your church to interview your young members. Help them find their motivational gifts from the Lord. Use surveys and questionnaires to help in a practical way to identify giftings and talents. Ask them, "What would you like to do for the Lord? What are some things you love doing? What has the Lord put in your heart

to do?" Or, "What would you like to do for the Lord in the near future, but need help in getting started?"

4. One thing we have done at Word of Life Centre is to make a list of all the members in the youth group and beside each name record the things they are involved in. Have a goal to make sure everyone has something to do.

5. Teach them that everything they do in ministry is for the Lord and for spreading the gospel. Tell them about the great rewards in serving Jesus. Mark 10:29-30 teaches us that whatever we sacrifice for the Lord or for the gospel will be rewarded a hundredfold "now" and in the age to come with eternal life.

6. Make up a list of all the ministry possibilities you can think of in which teenagers can serve. There are so many things they could do. All youth groups have dozens of things they can involve people in—from leading songs to playing instruments; from planning out activities to organizing different events. In our church we have more than 90 ministries in which young people can find a meaningful place of involvement. These areas of ministry include such things as: nursery, children's church, choir, drama, nursing homes, and feeding the poor.

7. Invite young people to participate in all your planning and brainstorming times. Sometimes the best ideas come from the people who are sitting in the youth group. They know what is needed in the group. Most of them know exactly what can be done to liven up the group or to reach out to their unsaved peers, possibly even better than the youth leader. Most of the time we don't see the gold mine we have sitting right in front of us. Some young people, between the ages of 13 and 18, know how to lead a youth group better than anyone else. They have sat in church meetings for years. They know where their generation is at.

They know what gets through to them and how to relate to them. They even know more Bible than they themselves realize.

A good way to get your workers to take more responsibility is to simply not tell them all of your ideas, but to sit back and let them come up with the ideas. Steer the brainstorming session to arrive at what you know needs to be done. This helps them feel that they are important and have input. The most important thing is the fact that when they give their suggestions, they will be more ready to get behind the project and do the work.

8. One way to involve others, in fact, one of my personal favorites, is to ask youth to help do an illustrated sermon or skits and dramas that fit with the theme of the service. Even shy teenagers come out of their shells when they can hide behind masks or costumes and act.

Christianity is not dull and boring! Church can be exciting, but many don't realize it. Involvement and participation helps us enjoy church more. One thing that really bothers me as I invite unsaved young people to church is their fear of boredom. This attitude could be one of the greatest hindrances to young people coming to your youth group and church. Young people hate going anywhere that is boring or merely gives the impression that it could be boring.

When you tell them church is the most exciting place to be, they don't believe you. Young people find it hard to believe that God has something exciting for them. Many teenagers today do not know a thing about God's plan for them. I boldly declare to them that God does have great and exciting things for them. Jesus came to give life and to give it abundantly (see Jn. 10:10). In His presence is fullness of joy (see Ps. 16:11). There are a lot of ways to bait the fishhook. In addition to all this is the joy of doing His will, being used by God, and feeling the anointing of God flow through you to touch people who need the Lord.

9. Tell them that God wants them on His team. If you ever had the chance to play alongside the greatest hockey player in the world, it would be incredible. It would be overwhelming, like a dream come true. What greater thrill could there be than to be a co-worker with Jesus, the Greatest of the greatest, and for Him to pick you to be on His team? Talk about a thrill of a lifetime! When Jesus invited Peter and Andrew to come follow Him, they immediately dropped their fishing nets and followed Him (see Mt. 4:19-20).

Training Up Champions

I love the story of Goliath-killer David when he was temporarily hiding in the cave of Adullam, in First Samuel 22. Four hundred men came to him in desperation. These men had problems. They were distressed, discontented, and in debt. All their problems started with the letter "D"; let's face it, these guys were "3-D" losers. It was a sad situation. But David took them in and he became a captain over them. Here is where this story gets exciting! David molded these men into champions. Four of them became giant-killers just like David (see 2 Sam. 21:15-22). A list of others and the exploits they did are in Second Samuel 23:8-39; almost an entire chapter is devoted to the great feats they accomplished! For example, Adino killed 800 men at one time! It all started with David taking and believing in the army that God gave him to start with.

You have a youth group full of potential. Every person is a potential worker who wants to be used by God. Be a champion like David! God will send you some needy young people—the world is full of them now more than ever. As they hang around with you and listen to you preach, counsel them, and build them up strong in God, they will become champions too. Don't be blind to whom God is calling and choosing to be part of His army.

Maybe you are saying, "I have diamonds in the rough, and it's going to take a long time for them to become something." Not necessarily! I have seen God do a fast work in people's lives. Some people in the Bible were water baptized, spoke in tongues, and prophesied all in one day (see Acts 19:5-6).

Chapter 4

Jehu: Zeal in Action

Jehu was an aggressive, zealous person who responded to the call of God on his life, became part of God's army, and did great exploits. He is an example for us on how to get red-hot for God! God commended him for what he did. Second Kings 10:30 states that God released such a blessing on Jehu that his sons sat on the throne of Israel for the next four generations. (But that's the end of the story.)

The Story of Jehu (2 Kings 9)

One day Jehu was sitting around with the other soldiers in the army when suddenly, one of the sons of the prophets came running in looking for a man named Jehu. This wild young prophet took Jehu into an inner room, poured a pitcher of oil on his head, and gave him a word from God. God spoke through this young prophet that He was anointing Jehu to be the next king of Israel to replace Jezebel and Ahab. Not only was he to dethrone them, but he also was to kill them and all their family and their officials. All the people were afraid of this wicked queen, Jezebel. She had killed thousands of God's prophets.

From that time on Jehu became a radical man for God. He believed the word and so did his friends. After hearing what the young prophet said, they believed it was from the Lord and conducted a quick coronation service to proclaim Jehu king. As soon as his friends laid down their garments on the tops of the steps and blew the trumpet to announce him as king of Israel, Jehu was on his way. Jehu, totally revolutionized by these events, rose up and went forth with great zeal and boldness.

Jehu was a man with promptness of action. He didn't wait around, but rose up to the challenge and began to do what God told him with all the energy, determination, and zeal that he had.

He charged against the enemies of the Lord and Israel with a fierceness and thoroughness. He was bold, daring, and masterful in strategy. He completely fulfilled every word spoken over him.

Jehu Drove His Chariot Furiously (2 Kings 9:20)

Jehu jumped into his chariot and headed straight for King Joram. The Bible says that he drove furiously. What an incredible fire and zeal he had to do exploits for the Lord.

Jehu was like the young David who went to meet Goliath. David didn't creep or crawl in fear to where Goliath was. The Bible says that David *ran* to meet with Goliath (see 1 Sam. 17:48). When teenagers get a word from God, get on fire, and possess the zeal and the drive that God places in them, they are remarkable to behold.

When do you drive furiously? "All the time," some of you might reply. Some would say, "I like the fast lane. I want to get where I am going as fast as I can." Others say, "I can't stand going slow or following behind a slow car. I have to pass them."

I don't condone speeding or reckless driving, but spiritually speaking, we are to serve God furiously. Our work for the Lord must never lag in zeal (see Rom. 12:11

NIV). If others are going slow, we can't let them hinder us. If others don't want to serve God in red-hot, boiling zeal, then pass them. You need to be a Christian who is growing in God and doing things for Him as best you can.

Why do people speed? Maybe some are running late and need to catch up. Maybe they have someone injured with them in the car and are rushing to take them to the hospital. Police, ambulance drivers, and others can speed because they have something important to do.

Jehu drove furiously. He had something important to do. The nation was in crisis. Jezebel had reigned long enough! He had the word of the Lord and the command of God. We too need to move when God tells us to move.

The Gospel of Mark records the life of Jesus much like a newspaper would. It is full of adverbs and action and other techniques that make the story sound exciting. "Straightway" Jesus did this; "immediately" Jesus did that. Jesus was an active person. Satan had had people bound in sickness for too long. Jesus had a mission and was zealous in performing what He had to do.

God is looking for people of action who want to do something great for Him. God chose Jehu because He needed someone who would act in zeal and haste and overthrow the house of Ahab.

Jehu Pulled Back His Bow With All His Strength

Now Jehu drew his bow with full strength and shot Jehoram between his arms; and the arrow came out at his heart, and he sank down in his chariot (2 Kings 9:24).

Jehu was not lukewarm! He didn't pull back his bow halfheartedly. He put all he had into what he was doing.

I don't think Joram was so far away that Jehu needed to pull back the bow that drastically. So why did he pull back the bow so hard that the arrow went right through Joram?

Jehu wanted to do more than just injure him. He was going to finish Joram off because it had been prophesied that Jehu would kill him.

Jehu was intense. He was a finisher. He made sure every task was done. Likewise, we are not called to do a little damage to the devil and the works of darkness. We need to go after the demonic forces that are holding people in darkness, sin, and sickness, and totally destroy them with the weapons of the Spirit that God puts in our hands.

Then Jehu continued his pursuit of the household of Ahab. The next relative was Ahaziah, King of Judah (see 2 Kings 9:27). Ahaziah, the nephew of Joram and of the bloodline of Jezebel, had been reigning for one year. He was as evil as Ahab. Jehu said, "Shoot him also in the chariot."

The next challenge was a tough one. All the people were afraid of the great Jezebel. She had killed thousands of God's prophets. Even Elijah was driven to depression when he knew that Jezebel wanted his death (see 1 Kings 19). But Jehu charged into town acting like he was going shopping and Jezebel was next on the list. Jezebel heard about his coming, put on her make-up, looked through the window at Jehu, and yelled down a threat. Jehu calmly called up to the window, "Whoever is on my side, throw her out" (see 2 Kings 9:32-33). Two or three eunuchs were on Jehu's side and tossed her out the window. Then Jehu went to have some lunch (see 2 Kings 9:34).

When we get the anointing, the touch of God, and a word of direction from God, the greatest enemies and the hardest tasks become like bread to us. Jehu, our example, wasn't intimidated by anyone either.

But you shall receive power when the Holy Spirit has come upon you; and you shall be witnesses to Me in Jerusalem,

and in all Judea and Samaria, and to the end of the earth
(Acts 1:8).

We have been given the power of the Holy Ghost. We
don't have to be intimidated by any of the enemies of God.
Jehu just spoke the word and Jezebel was overthrown. We
have power through the name of Jesus to do great things.
Greater is He who is in us than he that is in the world! (See
First John 4:4.)

Jehu's third assignment was the whole household of
Ahab. Jehu wrote letters this time to the rulers of Jezreel.
They were so terrified by the news of Jehu's killing two
other kings that they didn't want to fight with him. They
gave Jehu what he asked for—all the sons of Ahab. (See
Second Kings 10:1-5.)

Jehu had killed all of Ahab's family, his friends, private
chaplains, and finally, anyone who was close to him in any
way (see 2 Kings 10:11). On his way to Samaria, probably in
his chariot again, he met 42 relatives of the former king of
Judah, Ahaziah, and Jehu killed them too.

On the way to the next mission, as Jehu was charging
along, he met Jehonadab coming out to see him. I love this
little addition to the story (see 2 Kings 10:15-17). Jehu asked
Jehonadab, "Is your heart right, as my heart is toward your
heart?" He responded that it was. So Jehu said, "Give me
your hand." Jehu lifted him up into the chariot with him.
Jehu then said, "Come with me, and see my zeal for the
Lord." And Jehu, the Bible says, gave Jehonadab a ride in
his chariot.

As we live for God zealously, we will attract other
people. We can give them a lift up and take them for a ride
with us. We can take them with us and continue driving
zealously. Many people want to go for coffee with you and
be your friend, which is okay. However, nothing can beat

doing things for God together, or getting in our chariots and driving furiously to our next mission together as co-workers in the harvest. So Jehu and Jehonadab raced off in the chariot together to Jehu's next attack.

His fourth assignment was all the Baal worshipers. Jehu tricked all of the Baal worshipers into gathering together for a gigantic worship ceremony to Baal. All the Baal worshipers from all over the country came; they would have been stupid not to come to a celebration called by the new king. After they had all assembled in the room, Jehu's men killed every one of them. Then the soldiers totally destroyed everything that had to do with Baal worship and turned the empty building into a public toilet (see 2 Kings 10:27 TLB).

Jehu meant business! He was called to cut off the house of Ahab. *Cut off* in the margin of my Bible means "to destroy." We are called to destroy all the things that hinder our lives in God. Jehu, the "zealous destroyer," destroyed every trace of Baal from Israel.

Satan knows that he is in trouble when a zealous Christian comes out against him in holy anger to pull down his strongholds.

Zealous Christianity

Zeal accomplishes! Zeal is the inner drive to accomplish. Nothing is as exciting as having a zeal for the Lord. Are you experiencing zeal in your Christian walk? It is an essential quality for performing exploits.

What Is Zeal?

Zeal is delight, enjoyment, enthusiasm, excitement, fervor, fire, gusto, and zest. Zeal is to be fervent. To be fervent is to be red-hot. It is to be emotional, aroused, intense, flaming, feverish, turned on, powerful, and strong.

Some of you might be asking, "How can I get more zeal?" Throughout this entire book I want to help you to become more on fire for God and to spread a fire of zeal to everyone you can.

Let me give you a few clear points to help improve your "zeal level" right now. First, you must press in and meet with the Lord regularly. Ask the Lord to carry you into His presence and transform you. On the Day of Pentecost, 120 people met with God in the upper room and fire sat on each of them. I believe God's fire will fall on all of us as we continue to meet with Him. Second, ask God for the baptism of the Holy Ghost as on the Day of Pentecost. Then continue to stay full. Ephesians 5:18 says, "And do not be drunk with wine...but be filled with the Spirit." The Greek rendering of Ephesians 5:18 says, "continue to be being filled with the Spirit."

I believe Jehu's encounter with God in the inner room birthed a zeal in his heart. Before the encounter he sat around doing nothing, but after the anointing with oil, he became fervent. Meeting with God puts the fire of God on our heads and in our hearts.

Third, ask God to open the Word of God to you. In Luke 24:13-35 is an account of two men on the road to Emmaus. As they talked with Jesus and as He opened the Scriptures to them, their hearts began to burn. We today must have a strong daily time in the Word of God. Most people I talk to who have lost their zeal have one thing in common—they did not read their Bible regularly. Have quality times in the Bible every day and ask the Spirit to bring it alive to your heart.

...Therefore be zealous and repent (Revelation 3:19).

Fourth, we are to be zealous and repent. Our response to God's conviction should be one of zeal. If we have sinned, that sin cancels out our zeal. We must repent before the fire of God can return in our lives. Make a decision to be more zealous regarding the things of God and the things God asks you to do. Fifth, decide to be a zealous kind of person. If necessary, come against the strongholds of laziness and slothfulness in your life. Decide not to be lukewarm in any area of your life. In many verses the Bible teaches us that we are to have zeal and to have a zealous response. It implies that such is our decision. Decide to be zealous—start right now.

> *Never lag in zeal and in earnest endeavor; be aglow and burning with the Spirit, serving the Lord* (Romans 12:11 AMP).

We are to never let our zeal slip away from us. Always keep your *zeal*. Never lose it. It is possible to lose your zeal, to misplace it, or to forget about it. Even on our days off we are not to lag in zeal. Never let yourself slip into moods of laziness and sloth. You can have creative times of relaxation and refreshment, but never lag in zeal.

We are to never run out of zeal as a major, inner motivating factor in our lives. We are to never slow down in our burning passion for the Lord, never become slack in eagerness, or never be weary in the activity of youth ministry. Let's never lag behind in diligence, never be lazy in our work.

Lukewarm Christianity is so unfulfilling. There is nothing like having a zeal that burns for the Lord. It gives you vision. It fuels the drive that motivates you for the Lord and pushes you from within. It is not external, forced, legalistic motivation. It is the delight in serving the Lord.

We need this drive and vision from the Lord for more than just natural things. It's okay to get excited about natural things (when they aren't sinful, of course), but nothing beats getting excited for the Lord.

A burned-out Christian is a Christian who no longer has fire. Their flames are burned out. Romans 12:11 says that we are not to let that happen; we are to stay "aglow and burning" (AMP). It is sin to not stay on fire for God. It is nobody's fault but our own. Being burned-out is not being overworked. Burned-out people start to lose the energy and drive they need to accomplish the tasks at hand. I saw a tee shirt recently that said, "You don't need a holiday—you just need adventure."

Sixth, we can pray and ask God for more zeal. "Lord, put a new zeal in my heart for the lost, for the Word of God, and for prayer, and let it burn. Lord, give me a fresh desire for youth ministry. Lord, renew the call and the desire. Lord, renew the desire for Your presence."

Christians can start feeling weary and even start missing church. They start losing their desire for the things of God. Right after I first became a Christian, I remember meeting a young, on-fire teenage girl in the church that I had started attending. Her excitement about going to church stirred me. She said, "I would never miss Young People's for the world!" I could see that she was excited about what was happening in her youth group. That attracted me. I had to find out what was so exciting about church that she would not miss it.

We can get so on fire that people will come just to watch us burn. Young people are attracted to zeal. You can get a movement going in your youth group that will stir many others because of the blaze in your heart. They will come up to you and say, "Can I come with you as you burn for Jesus today?" Then you can give them a lift into your chariot and go perform some great exploits.

We are to come out from among the people and be different. If everyone else is lazy, don't you be. Instead be different and separate yourself (see 2 Cor. 6:17). Be an example of what a normal Christian should be like.

We need to out-give, out-pray, and out-evangelize what we did for God last year with a zeal that is burning brighter and brighter. In fact, we need to have such a Jehu anointing that we will out-give, out-pray, and out-evangelize most Christians today. This is what normal Christianity really is.

To be different means to be "opposite, distinct, varying, unequal, unlike, unmatched." Wow! We are not to be conformed to this world (see Rom. 12:2). We are not to live in the lukewarm, backslidden state we see all around us. We need to be the risk-takers who rise up, who are different, and who do something great for God.

Don't Slow Down

The saddest portion of Jehu's story is his failure to destroy the golden calves that were at Bethel and Dan (see 2 Kings 10:29). I don't know what happened at that point. Maybe he thought he had done enough. Many Christians can sit back and say, "I did my quota of evangelism when I was young. Boy, did I burn for the Lord, but now I am more mature and wise." We need to keep our spiritual zeal as we get older. We need to zealously deal with every sin in our lives and continue to do exploits.

As you go for God, there will always be those who come and say you are doing too much, that you had better slow down. Now, we all need to be open to input and correction from others, but we also need to make sure that the advice is not coming from a backslidden saint feeling guilty because he isn't as zealous as we are. So don't let anything slow you down. Don't let satan, sin, or saints slow you down.

One Friday night I was out street evangelizing with a crowd of about 20 of our teenagers. We closed in on a youth hangout. A man came driving over to where we were talking to some teenagers and started to scorch me for pushing Christianity on others. I listened and held back from getting into an argument with him, as he continued to blast me for our style of evangelism. When he was done, I asked, "Sir, do you see that group over there? They are our young people and about twenty sinners are listening to them. See that other group there and there?" I pointed to about five different groups of our young people. "These young people need the Lord and are listening to what we are saying. Be careful that you don't try to discourage something that God is using." I could have said, "I like my way of evangelizing better than your way of not evangelizing," but I didn't.

Long-Term Zeal

Sadly, Jehu is an example of only short-term zeal. He is not a great example of having long-term zeal. We need to have zeal, but it should be a zeal that lasts longer than several short spurts.

Jesus is our flawless example in all areas. For instance, one day the disciples saw Jesus cleansing the temple in zeal, and the Bible says, "Then His disciples remembered that it was written, 'Zeal for Your house has eaten Me up' " (Jn. 2:17). Even though there are great stories in the Bible of great men, all of them still had weaknesses. Only Jesus is our perfect hero in all areas.

Another thing that really helps me with my zeal is the input of others. The Bible teaches us in Hebrews 3:13 to "exhort one another daily, while it is called 'Today,' lest any of you be hardened through the deceitfulness of sin." We all need the input of others—daily. We need others around us who can give us daily encouragement, those who in low seasons notice that we are slowing down a bit and stir us to zeal. Every one of us needs this Scripture—whether we are preachers, parents, or just strong Christians. We all need around us those who have zeal. You need to be a person who can stir up the zeal in young people. The King James Version of Second Corinthians 9:2 says, "…your zeal hath provoked very many."

We not only need to stir them toward zeal; we also need to provoke them. Some definitions of provoke are to "aggravate, excite, upset, make jealous, poke or prod into action."

I remember, as a young farm boy, always having hundreds of pigs. It was an enormous challenge to get the pigs to walk up the ramp into the truck. Many times we used a "pig prod." It was a hollow metal cylinder that held about ten "D" batteries. We would face the pigs in the right direction and then come behind them and give them a few volts in the rear. Sometimes they would stand and squeal, but usually it worked and they ran up the ramp.

Sometimes a gentle prod from the Holy Ghost or from a godly friend is needed to get us going for Him. This was what the Lord did to Jehu. Jehu was just sitting around with his friends, possibly discussing the battle and what should be done. Perhaps he was just sitting in discouragement, wondering why more wasn't being done. Then Jehu was sprung into action by the Holy Ghost.

Getting young people on fire for God is your primary task! If we can get young people into the inner room, get them meeting with God, minister to them the Holy Ghost oil and fire, get them going in zeal for the Lord, then the guaranteed result will be exploits for the Lord. They will know God. They will be strong. They will be inspired by the Lord to do exploits.

Chapter 5

Keys to Transformation

What made the difference in Jehu's life? One moment he is sitting around and the next moment he is jumping onto his chariot and driving like a wild man. Maybe his friends were asking the same question. You can imagine what shock they experienced when a madman suddenly came running in where they were sitting with Jehu and ordered him into the inner room!

Then, when Jehu came out, they asked him, "Why did this madman come to you?" (2 Kings 9:11) Jehu tried to avoid the question, but with the oil dripping from his head, they knew something had happened. I also believe that they saw something different about Jehu.

When I was growing up, all I knew about church was that it was a boring place to go. Church is boring unless you meet God there. Religion is boring. Meeting with God and having Him meet with you and talk to you is life-transforming. Think about the glow on Moses' face after he had met with God (see Ex. 34:29). There is definitely nothing boring about meeting with God.

And it shall come to pass in the last days, says God, that I will pour out of My Spirit on all flesh; your sons and

*your daughters shall prophesy, your young men shall
see visions, your old men shall dream dreams. And on
My menservants and on My maidservants I will pour out
My Spirit in those days; and they shall prophesy* (Acts
2:17-18).

It is God's will to meet with young people and to pour
out His Spirit on them. Youth workers need to believe God
for these verses to come to pass in their youth ministry.
Having an invasion of the power of God is vital because it is
that power that transforms young lives and complete youth
groups.

Jehu was taken into a room away from his friends to be
alone with the prophetic anointing and the message from
God. Then the oil was poured on his head. These things are
all important to the transformation of Jehu.

*...make him arise up from among his brethren, and **carry**
him to an inner chamber* (2 Kings 9:2 KJV).

The young prophet was to get Jehu into an inner chamber, even if he had to carry him. The inner chamber is a type
of worship and the presence of God. Everyone must meet
with God in the inner room like Jehu before they can do exploits. God also seeks worshipers to meet with Him.

*But the hour is coming, and now is, when the true wor-
shipers will worship the Father in spirit and in truth; for
the Father is **seeking** such to worship Him* (John 4:23).

God is seeking for young people to worship Him in
spirit and in truth. God, the mighty God in Heaven, is seeking for people who will really worship Him. How can we
encourage young people to enter the inner chamber of worship? Let us consider three alternatives.

1. The Nebuchadnezzar Approach to Worship

You, O king, have made a decree that everyone who hears the sound of the horn, flute, harp, lyre, and psaltery, in symphony with all kinds of music, shall fall down and worship the gold image (Daniel 3:10).

King Nebuchadnezzar erected a huge golden image and commanded everyone to fall down and worship it as soon as all the music began to play. Daniel 3:6 says, "And whoever does not fall down and worship shall be cast immediately into the midst of a burning fiery furnace."

Nebuchadnezzar's method of getting the people to worship his gods and this golden image was to make decrees, commands, and threats. This may be somewhat of a farfetched example, but can you imagine a youth worker leading songs and trying to get young people to worship God using Nebuchadnezzar's style? "Teens, I want you to lift your hands right now! You start singing! All of you will worship God or else. Now I am going to start singing this song again, and you had better begin to sing and do what I tell you or I will send you to the pastor's office!"

Of course nobody would do something like that—but we need to be careful that we don't try to force young people to worship God in youth meetings. This is not the style of worship that God wants. God doesn't have to use threats or intimidation to get worship; neither should we use these methods to force young people into worship.

God doesn't use legalism, guilt tactics, or religious bondage to force us to worship Him. This style motivates people to worship out of fear rather than love.

2. Satan's Approach to Worship

Again, the devil took Him up on an exceedingly high mountain, and showed Him all the kingdoms of the world and their glory. And he said to Him, "All these things I will give You if You will fall down and worship me" (Matthew 4:8-9).

Satan's way to get worship from Jesus was by using trickery and offering rewards. Satan offered Jesus things that he thought might tempt Jesus. Satan offered all the kingdoms of this world, if only Jesus would bow down and worship him.

God will never use trickery to fool us into worshiping Him. He will not bribe us with all the blessings He could give us. Neither should youth leaders resort to this style of bribery to encourage young people to worship God. We shouldn't ever offer rewards to young people for falling down and worshiping God in a youth meeting.

It is important to include here also about the battle satan is advancing against young people to steal their worship from God as he tried with Jesus. He still delivers the same offer to teens today. Satan offered all he had (all the kingdoms of the world) to Jesus, and he is still ready to offer all he has in order to steal the worship we are giving to God.

We need to continually remind young people to be aware of satan's strategies. We must encourage them to set their affections on things above and not to put their affections on the things of earth with which satan tempts us (see Col. 3:2). Teach young people to address the demon forces with the strength and conviction of the Word of God as Jesus did. "Then Jesus said to him, 'Away with you, Satan! For it is written, "You shall worship the Lord your God, and Him only you shall serve" ' " (Mt. 4:10).

3. The Love Approach

God wants to win us over to His love. God's approach is a free invitation. We don't *have* to worship God; we *get* to! We are invited to His banquet. We, as the Church, are His Bride, His lover. The Song of Solomon describes our relationship with God as the story of two lovers. God is inviting us to His banqueting table and His banner over us is love (see Song 2:4). *God wants to capture our hearts and win us over with His love.*

Once God's love draws us and we meet God, we are changed! His love changes us. Something happens to us as we are in His powerful presence. Even a dead stick placed before God's presence comes alive.

*And Moses placed the rods before the Lord in the tabernacle of witness. ...behold, the rod of Aaron, of the house of Levi, had **sprouted** and put forth **buds**, had produced **blossoms** and yielded **ripe almonds*** (Numbers 17:7-8).

God is a master at taking things we think are dead and useless and causing them to come to life. They will start sprouting, putting forth buds, getting some blossoms, and producing ripe fruit. This was in a time frame of just overnight. God can do things overnight when we get into His Presence or get His presence into us and our youth meetings.

If you are working with young people who are dead to the things of God, there is still hope. If your youth meetings are dragging and going nowhere, evaluate if the Lord is there. Is God in what you are doing? Seek the Lord for His power and blessing behind your ministry. You are the key for a new spark of God!

Praise and worship with young people can be very exciting and fun. Young people love music. There are so many styles of music to express our devotion to the Lord. There are always dozens of new songs available to draw from to add life and zest.

Variety is a major key. An assortment of different songs and diverse packages of praise and worship songs are important. The best songs can quickly become tiresome and boring. Youth meetings need variety from week to week and something totally different from Sunday services.

Teach Young People to Be Worshipers

1. Teach them by example. Leading young people in worship is possible only when we ourselves are worshipers. We must lead the way in ascending up the hill of the Lord to His presence.

2. We must teach young people that worship is more than just singing songs, and definitely more than just singing slow songs. Worship in the Old Testament meant to surrender to God. As we surrender our lives more to God, we enter into a greater worship experience with God. Abraham's taking his son Isaac to Mount Moriah to sacrifice him to the Lord is one of the greatest displays of worship in the Bible (see Gen. 22). As we lay our lives down in surrender to God, God sees that as worship to Him (see Rom. 12:1 NIV).

3. Teach on the style and forms of expression of praise that God likes. There are all manner of instruments and many forms of expression with our bodies, including singing, shouting, clapping, lifting of the hands, bowing, standing, dancing, and clapping. Come into His presence with singing and thankfulness. Rejoice in the Lord.

There are many different meanings for the word *rejoice*, but one is "to spin." "Let the earth rejoice" really means, "let the earth spin," and so it does. It also means "to leap with the feet, to move around, to stamp, to spring about wildly for joy." God wants us to rejoice in Him; to spin and move around as we offer up praise to Him.

4. Teach them to worship because He is worthy (see Rev. 4:11). He is the great Creator of the universe and is worthy of my raising my hand in the air, or my voice singing a praise song. He is worthy of my entire life. We don't need any feelings; we worship because He is God—a fact!

5. Teach them to worship God because we were created to worship. If we don't worship God, we will worship something or someone else. He is most worthy of our worship!

6. Teach them to worship because ours is a love relationship with God. I worship God because He is God, but I also worship God because I love Him and love being near Him. Yes, there are great *feelings* too!

In the New Testament, the Greek word for *worship* has a more intimate meaning than that of surrender to the Lord. It means "to kiss." We can have a close, intimate, growing relationship with God. As we draw near to God, God will draw near to us. It is a wonderful thing for God to invite us into the inner chamber to be close and intimate with Him.

One day I saw a vision that I believe was from the Lord. I saw myself worshiping God in Heaven with thousands and thousands of people—a massive crowd of people in zealous music and song before God. As I continued worshiping, I closed my eyes. When I opened them, I was all alone with the Lord. So to me, Heaven will be worshiping with the multitude, yet being alone with God in a precious love relationship.

7. Teach them to worship because of the benefits of worship. My favorite time of meeting God with young people is on Tuesday mornings. We have taken an hour to meet with God every Tuesday for many years. One of the theme Scriptures for that time has been Acts 13:2: "As they ministered to the Lord and fasted, the Holy Spirit said...." We come to worship, to adore, and to minister to Him. Then He speaks prophetically to us.

Worshiping God is a major principle behind everything that happens in our church. It is the key for our hearing God's voice of direction. It is the key to every visitation we have ever had.

But the people who know their God shall be strong, and carry out great exploits (Daniel 11:32b).

A close relationship with God is the key to our strength! It is essential for everyone who wants to do exploits to go into the inner room. The inner room is the only path to exploits. Jehu met with God in the inner chamber and it changed his life forever!

Baptism of the Holy Ghost

Jehu's inner room experience was similar to what happened to Peter and the other 119 in the upper room on the Day of Pentecost. It is a life-changing experience to receive the baptism of the Holy Spirit.

Next to getting saved, the baptism of the Holy Ghost was the most thrilling and life-changing event that ever happened to me. The power of Pentecost—the power of being full of the Holy Ghost—is vital for every Christian. It is impossible to do exploits without the Holy Ghost's empowering.

Paul, a world-changing New Testament hero, gave us his key to his being so powerful. "I thank my God I speak with tongues more than you all" (1 Cor. 14:18).

Youth leaders and parents need to teach young people about the baptism of the Holy Ghost and the power of speaking in tongues. After you feel you have explained this gift of God enough, then believe that everyone who wants it, receives it as you lay hands on them. I personally love praying with people to receive the power of the Holy Ghost.

Occasionally some might not receive immediately. My experience with receiving the baptism was very frustrating. For four long months I sought the baptism but never got a breakthrough with a prayer language of tongues. This was good in one sense, in that I could identify and help others with the same problem. I have patience and faith for people to receive.

One reason it took me so long was that I didn't have enough teaching. It is not always essential to have teaching to receive the Holy Ghost, for many times people get saved and baptized in the Holy Ghost in that same prayer. Most times, however, it is important to explain the promise that God has for them.

As you teach, try to make things as easy to understand as possible. I like using Acts 2:4 in The Living Bible: "And everyone present was filled with the Holy Spirit and began speaking in languages they didn't know, for the Holy Spirit gave them this ability." These 120 people were all filled with the Holy Ghost and began to speak in tongues *as the Spirit gave them the words*. I state that the Holy Ghost comes in as soon as you ask (according to Lk. 11:13). But then you must open your mouth and begin to speak in tongues by faith. As you begin to speak, the Holy Ghost will give you the words of your new prayer language.

I like to use the phone as an illustration. People can have the phone installed and placed on the wall, but the wires need to be hooked up and plugged in. When we ask God for the baptism of the Holy Ghost, I believe He comes in, but then we need to plug the phone in and speak in tongues to make the final connection.

Another illustration I use is the water tap. We know there is water inside the pipes, but it isn't until we turn on the tap that some water flows out. After we pray and ask God to fill us, we have been filled with the Holy Ghost. However, as we begin to speak in tongues by faith, it is like turning on the tap. As we begin to turn the tap, a few drops come out, then a little stream. The more we turn the tap, the more the water comes out.

Another reason I had problems speaking in tongues was that I was very shy. As you pray with young people to receive the baptism, be sensitive to not embarrass them. Some people get all tense because others are watching them and they can't relax and focus on their prayer to the Lord.

Once I was preaching about the baptism of the Holy Spirit in a youth meeting held in a big house. The power of God came down so strongly that everyone received the Holy Ghost except for one certain young man. I looked around for a room where I could take him for some private prayer. It just happened that this house had a swimming pool and I ended up taking this young man into the changing room. I asked him whom he felt comfortable with enough to join us for prayer, and he wanted his youth pastor and his best friend.

The four of us went into the men's changing room. The key for this young man was to get him alone, answer his questions, and give a little more explanation until he had faith and was ready to receive. I then led him in a prayer like this: "Lord, thank You for saving me and thank You for Your promise that You would fill me with the Holy Ghost. Jesus, I ask You to baptize me with the Holy Spirit with the evidence of speaking with tongues."

Immediately the power of God fell aggressively on him. He flew against the wall of the changing room and his prayer language came out like a gusher. As he crashed into the wall, his head just missed two hooks on the wall that were used to hang up clothes. The power of God came on him, gave him his prayer language, and directed his head to miss those hooks. It was a glorious time as we continued speaking in tongues in the men's changing room.

That night was the first night of a youth weekend. God went on to totally transform that youth group from one of apathy and carnality to one of fire and zeal.

Another important thing to look for in praying for young people to get filled with the Holy Ghost is "hunger." Hunger is one of the most important ingredients to receiving the baptism. Teach young people how to get hungry.

Blessed are those who hunger and thirst for righteousness, for they shall be filled (Matthew 5:6).

..."If anyone thirsts, let him come to Me and drink. He who believes in Me, as the Scripture has said, out of his heart will flow rivers of living water." But this He spoke concerning the Spirit, whom those believing in Him would receive... (John 7:37-39).

On another occasion, I was invited to teach on the baptism of the Holy Ghost by a pastor who had recently received the baptism of the Spirit and was anxious to get his entire youth group filled.

I taught for about an hour, explaining all the Scriptures about salvation and the baptism of the Spirit. I shared on such verses as Acts 2:38, and I told them that the promise of the Holy Ghost was for all. I asked, "Who wants to receive this promise from the Lord today?" All 30 of them raised their hands. This time I just asked them to stay seated—as in the Book of Acts, chapter 2. I led them in a prayer and then went around to each one, laying my hands on their heads as the Bible teaches. It was a glorious time. God moved in and totally changed that youth group as every one of them received the baptism.

I particularly remember one young man. As I laid my hands on him, he instantly started to loudly speak in tongues. It was a peculiar tongue and very funny. Everyone in the room heard him and started to rejoice with laughter and the joy of the Lord as they saw what God was doing.

This young man, who was about 16 years old, was totally lost in God. With tears of joy pouring down his face, he continued speaking in tongues for more than an hour, oblivious to anyone else. In fact, I began preaching again, explaining a bit more about what God was doing. I had to speak quite loudly for everyone to hear because he still had rivers of living water pouring out of him. I love seeing God move on young people—it is one of the greatest keys for a move of God.

The Prophetic Message in the Inner Chamber

Then he arose and went into the house. And he poured the oil on his head, and said to him, "Thus says the Lord God of Israel: 'I have anointed you king over the people of the Lord, over Israel' " (2 Kings 9:6).

To complete these thoughts on Jehu's transformation, I want to include a discussion of the power of the prophetic word from God spoken over people's lives.

The young prophet poured the oil on Jehu's head and prophesied. Having taken the oil from Elisha and the words of prophecy that were given him to say, he did what he was told. An impartation was completed through the channel of the young unnamed prophet.

From that time on, Jehu was a different man. When people hear from God, it changes their lives. The prophetic message changed Jehu for life. He became a mighty warrior and king for the Lord. The prophetic anointing burst Jehu into the call of God for his life. He ran furiously! He drew the bow back with all his strength.

Our goal is to help young people fulfill their destinies. As we lay our hands on the young people and commission them, they will arise and become champions for Jesus! I believe God wants to grip this generation with a dynamic move of His Spirit that will make them rise up from among their brethren to do a work for the Lord.

For I long to see you, that I may impart to you some spiritual gift, so that you may be established (Romans 1:11).

Here Paul was longing to go to Rome to impart spiritual gifts. Getting spiritual gifts, according to this Scripture, was another way of bringing a solid establishment into their lives.

This charge I commit to you, son Timothy, according to the prophecies previously made concerning you, that by them you may wage the good warfare (1 Timothy 1:18).

Timothy, the young pastor, had received words of prophecy given to him by prophets. In this passage Paul shares a principle with us of how powerful prophetic words are in our warfare, or in the exploits that God has called us to do.

When the prophets laid hands on Timothy, God flowed through the prophets and gave him additional anointing and giftings to perform supernatural exploits and ministry for the glory of God.

Paul also was encouraging Timothy to give himself wholly to meditation on the actual words that were spoken over him (see 1 Tim. 4:14-15). As he gave himself to serious meditation, praying those words over and over, they would help him grow and improve in his spiritual progress.

Paul tells us to covet the gifts of the Spirit, especially the gift of prophecy, because it builds up and benefits people (see 1 Cor. 14:1). I am a believer in the gift of prophecy for today's local church.

This subject can be scary to those who have never had God use them in this way, or strange to those who have never seen it. It could be a cause for great reservation on the part of those who have seen the gift abused. Paul tells us very clearly to judge prophecy and to ensure it is given with proper leadership oversight.

We are not to despise, think lightly, or demean the gift of prophecy. Nor are we to quench the Spirit (see 1 Thess. 5:19-20). Some of the great benefits of the gift of prophecy are seen in First Corinthians 14:3-4 in the Amplified Bible.

> *...the one who prophesies [who interprets the divine will and purpose...] speaks to men for their **upbuilding** and **constructive spiritual progress** and **encouragement** and **consolation**. ...he who prophesies...**edifies** and **improves the church** and **promotes growth** [in...holiness, and happiness]* (1 Corinthians 14:3-4 AMP).

The gifts of the Spirit are so important in raising young people!

May I go a step further? Not only do we stir up the gifts of the Spirit ourselves, individually, but we also encourage the young people to believe for God to use them in the nine gifts of the Spirit as well (see 1 Cor. 12:8-10). This creates a great spiritual desire for the Lord and the moving of His Spirit in all of our prayer meetings and rallies. *We expect* God to release these gifts in people. We seek God to come by His Spirit. *We expect* signs to follow the preaching of His word (see Mk. 16:20).

The Importance of Laying Hands on Young People

Lay hands on your young people as often as you can, imparting the blessing of God and gaining prophetic insights from the Lord every time you pray for them. Jesus Himself picked up children and blessed them (see Mk. 10:14-16). I believe in the laying on of hands and speaking God's blessing on young people.

> *Do not neglect the gift that is in you, which was given to you by prophecy with the laying on of the hands of the eldership. Meditate on these things; give yourself entirely to them, that your progress may be evident to all* (1 Timothy 4:14-15).

We lay hands on them to help them receive the baptism of the Spirit as well as the gifts of the Spirit (see Rom. 1:11).

We teach on the gifts of the Spirit and then have a workshop atmosphere afterward to believe the Lord to give gifts. For example, we teach on the gift of prophecy and then have whoever would like to receive the gift of prophecy come up for prayer. We encourage them to covet the gift of prophecy as the Bible instructs (see 1 Cor. 14:1,39 KJV). Then we lay hands on them and see them receive it.

God has given each of us the ability to do certain things well. So if God has given you the ability to prophesy, then prophesy whenever you can—as often as your faith is strong enough to receive a message from God (Romans 12:6 TLB).

I love that verse; it has helped me so much. Faith is a key element in moving in the gifts. God wants us to have faith to receive a prophecy to build up others.

A prophetic touch on our lives and on the youth group is invaluable. It is like having a current understanding of what God is saying and doing, like being up to date with God.

He who has an ear, let him hear what the Spirit says to the churches (Revelation 3:22).

We need a fresh prophetic mantle in order to call the young people into action. It takes prophetic leaders to move the church forward and advance the young people into the call of God.

In First Samuel 10, Samuel anointed Saul to be the first king of Israel and gave him a prophecy that the Spirit of God would come upon him and he would prophesy and be transformed into another man. Immediately, as Saul turned his back to leave, God gave him another heart (see 1 Sam. 10:9). As Saul went on his way, he met the company of the prophets and the Spirit of God came upon him so that he prophesied among them (see 1 Sam. 10:10). The prophetic anointing can come and totally change people's hearts.

Incredible changes happen when you get people into the inner courts of the Lord. Youth ministries need teaching on the anointing, how to lead worship songs, and how to draw young people into the presence of God. We need to get teenagers into the presence of God where God changes, calls, anoints, and empowers.

A Challenging Message

Chapter 6

The Challenge to Full Potential

So the young man, the servant of the prophet, went to Ramoth Gilead. And when he arrived, there were the captains of the army sitting; and he said, "I have a message for you, Commander." Jehu said, "For which one of us?" And he said, "For you, Commander" (2 Kings 9:4-5).

I want to discuss further the power of the prophetic message that the young prophet gave to Jehu. It was a prophetic challenge. We too must get a fresh word from God, a prophetic challenge, for our youth group and this generation! The message we get from God is powerful and transforming. We need to give it out again with full force and with all the anointing we can receive from God.

The young prophet had a word from God for Jehu. We today cannot simply play games and give divine suggestions. We must have a strong mandate and message to present, and then give it with all confidence and boldness.

Give Young People a Challenge

Someone once told me that young men need something more than just to be motivated or "fired up." This person said, "You can get someone excited or 'fired up,' but unless you are around to keep them fired up, the fire may die down or go completely out. The way to have a lasting impact on their lives is to give them a *challenge*."

That one piece of insight helped me so much. It started a new surge of life in my preaching and counseling, and in my approach to youth ministry. Young people need a challenge that will grip their hearts to stand up among their peers. Satan wants to keep them down, but God will raise up an army. With the proper motivation and the right help, young people will rise up to their callings.

Jehu, in my opinion, is a type of this young generation. We, as parents and youth ministers, need to find the people whom God is speaking to, lay our hands on them, and carry them into the inner chamber to meet with God.

People need a shake! They need others to come and present the gospel to them, to pray for them, and to *compel* them to come to the banquet that God has prepared for them.

The Gospel Is Challenging

For the preaching of the cross is to them that perish foolishness; but unto us which are saved it is the power of God (1 Corinthians 1:18 KJV).

I am a believer in strong preaching, preaching where the message of God is given in a clear effective way under the anointing of God. Paul declared that he was not ashamed of the gospel of Christ, for it is the power of God unto salvation (see Rom. 1:16).

In the story of Jehu, the young prophet gave Jehu a message from God with a boldness and authority that affected Jehu's entire life. In fact, it radically changed him and launched him into a totally new orbit for God.

Preachers today, no matter what age, need to get a message from God and deliver it with boldness to their young people, without a fear of rejection or a desire to be a crowd-pleaser (see Mt. 22:16 AMP).

Jesus was known to teach the way of God truthfully, regardless of consequences and without fear of man. He was impartial and did not regard either the person or the position of anyone.

> *Then Jesus said to His disciples, "If anyone desires to come after Me, let him deny himself, and take up his cross, and follow Me"* (Matthew 16:24).

The Challenge to Totally Follow God

Young people need to be challenged to live for God. They need to be challenged to be zealous, challenged with the call of God for their lives. When the rich young ruler asked Jesus what he should do to enter the Kingdom of God, Jesus answered, "...Go your way, sell whatever you have and give to the poor...and come, take up the cross, and follow Me" (Mk. 10:21). Jesus laid out the "Follow Me" message, plain and simple. Young people need to be challenged to the core of their beings. I am not talking about being cruel, hard-nosed, or offensive. The Bible tells us in this verse that Jesus looked on the young man and loved him, but still challenged him to lay down everything to follow Him.

The story goes on to say in the next verse that the rich man went away sorrowful because he had many riches. Jesus didn't run after him and say, "I'm sorry; maybe I was asking too much." Jesus didn't apologize for the challenge.

One of the greatest challenges for young people is to be confronted about being a Christian and following after God with all their hearts. Sometimes it isn't the most popular thing to become a Christian. Not only can old friends laugh at you, but the possibility of persecution and opposition can also come.

This could have been Jehu's situation. God was calling him to rise up from among his peers and to do something great for God—to stand up for God in his nation.

> *...go in and make him rise up from among his associates...*
> (2 Kings 9:2).

God has called us to influence young people to the point that they will stand up among their associates, brethren, and peers, and take a stand for God. When young people get over this hurdle, they will get excited about standing apart and being different. Young people have a desire for destiny and militancy. Assure them that God will be with them when they stand in front of their peers, when they stand before the Goliaths that will face them. Build faith and courage into them to stand for God boldly.

The Challenge to Be on Fire and to Really Live for God

Every youth group has different levels of spiritual growth. Most youth groups have teenagers who have been Christians for years. Some of these young people are on fire; others are boringly familiar with everything that goes on. Some of the youth group, hopefully, are brand-new to the faith. Others may be carnal or backslidden, but for some reason still attend. Many youth groups can even have a section that is super spiritual—almost legalistic and religious.

All these different teens pose a positive challenge to any youth ministry. Each of these need different input and ministry. However, the goal for each is to get them on fire for God. Develop a core group of young people who are strong, dedicated, and zealous. Then strive to increase that core until the majority of your group is on fire for God. Once you get a momentum of youth on fire, that fire can spread and consume the entire youth group.

Those who are wise shall shine like the brightness of the firmament, and those who turn many to righteousness like the stars forever and ever (Daniel 12:3).

How do you turn each of the different groupings into a core of committed young people passionate for God? It takes the wisdom of God. God will give you the wisdom you need to bring a separate challenge to each group of young people you minister to.

One of the best definitions of wisdom I ever heard is this: "Knowing and doing what is the absolute best in every situation." It really does take the wisdom of God to ignite young people for Him.

I love the story of Solomon where he was given the incredible task of leading the nation of Israel. It would have been hard enough to lead a nation at any time, let alone when following the greatest king ever, his father David. On top of that, David referred to Solomon as someone young and inexperienced, but as the one God had chosen to be the next king (see 1 Chron. 29:1).

Between being young, following King David's footsteps, and leading a nation, Solomon was probably wondering if he could do it all. There is nothing wrong about feeling unqualified for the job. God has ways of putting us into responsibilities where we need to trust Him, not our own abilities or talents. Maybe some of you are brand-new youth ministers. Maybe you too feel young and inexperienced, and that others around you seem more qualified than you. It is quite possible that there are others around you who are more talented and gifted to do it—but you are the one called for the job!

Solomon gave us a terrific example of what to do when we are put in a position of leadership that we don't feel capable of handling.

Now, O Lord my God, You have made Your servant king instead of my father David, but I am a little child; I do not know how to go out or come in. And Your servant is in the midst of Your people whom You have chosen, a great people, too numerous to be numbered or counted. Therefore give Your servant an understanding heart to judge Your people, that I may discern between good and evil. For who is able to judge this great people of Yours? (1 Kings 3:7-9)

Solomon prayed and asked God for wisdom and understanding in learning to deal with the people of God. The Bible says that God was pleased with what Solomon had asked (see 1 Kings 3:10). He could have asked for wealth and many other things, but he sought first the well-being of the nation. God loves it when our prayer life consists of more than "me, myself, and I," and we spend time praying for others.

And God gave Solomon wisdom and exceedingly great understanding, and largeness of heart like the sand on the seashore (1 Kings 4:29).

This is a verse we can claim when working with young people. God will not only give us wisdom, but also an exceeding amount of wisdom and a heart as great as the sand on the seashore. We need God's heart for people and the wisdom to influence and turn them to righteousness. It takes all we can get from God to impact young people and challenge them to do what God has called them to do.

The Challenge to Give All of Their Lives

So Jesus answered and said, "Assuredly, I say to you, there is no one who has left house or brothers or sisters or father or mother or wife or children or lands, for My sake and the gospel's, who shall not receive a hundredfold now in this time—houses and brothers and sisters and mothers and children and lands, with persecutions—and in the age to come, eternal life (Mark 10:29-30).

One thing our local congregation does is challenge our young people to give a portion of their summer holidays to evangelism opportunities. They can give a week, two weeks, a month, or all of their summer holidays to God. Many of them will only be bored for the summer, and this is an opportunity for them to have the best summer they ever had.

Every year the response is surprising. They come in the morning and have devotions as a corporate group, one to two hours of training on evangelism, and then go out to evangelism opportunities in the afternoons, evenings, and weekends.

After their graduation, we challenge teenagers to give a year of their lives to God, no matter what vocational area they want to pursue. They come to Bible College in the mornings and then, like the summer program, give their afternoons, evenings, and weekends to the work of the ministry. They go evangelizing on outreach teams, assist in the care ministries of the church, and much more. With this program, we encourage each student to gather sponsors and housing for an entire year.

The Challenge for Academic Excellence

One other area that I feel is absolutely essential to challenge young people in, is in their school grades and work habits.

I became a Christian at age 16, in grade 11. My average grade was 65 percent before I was saved. Just after I gave my life to Christ, my marks shot up 15 to 20 percent in every class. Without even consciously trying harder, Jesus was changing my value system and helping me. That was one of the ways I was able to witness to my classmates. Get saved and your marks will go higher!

When you give your life to Christ, you get the mind of Christ, and as you get into the Word of God, your mind gets renewed. As you start reading such verses as, "I can do all things through Christ who strengthens me" (Phil. 4:13), and actually believing it, your mentality changes. While in school, I continued to pray and ask God to help me as I faced exams, and He did.

As we dedicate the abilities He has given us to use for His glory, God helps us in unusual ways.

It bothers me when I see Christian young people satisfied with underachievement. They have the "brain frame" that school is not very important. We have had some young people who, because they were planning on attending Bible College immediately after high school, didn't think they needed to graduate with a university level education.

I believe that the primary responsibility for teenagers, outside of their commitment to the Lord and to their families, is their schoolwork. Schoolwork is the equivalent of an adult's job. If they are failing in their schoolwork, they are failing in one of their top priorities. They are planting seeds of failure that they will reap in their future. Young people need to be challenged in the area of their academic achievements, to multiply their talents and abilities.

Matthew 25:14-30 is one of the parables of the talents. One man was given five talents, another was given two, and a third was given one talent. Talents, in the text, refer to units of money (verse 15 of the Amplified Bible states that each talent was worth a thousand dollars). However, they serve as a foundation for what we are to do with all the gifts and giftings that God gives us. Romans 12:6 says, "Having then gifts differing according to the grace that is given to us...."

In relation to the area of academics, some people feel as if they have only one talent operating in their lives, and therefore feel condemned to stay at that level for the rest of their lives. However, I will never accept the thought that some students born with only one talent in relation to their intelligence have to stay at that level for the rest of their lives. We should never write people off as being slow or stupid.

In the same manner that the talents increased in the parable, every person, including young people, can increase, enlarge, and multiply their talents. People stay at one talent because they choose to. They are like the man with one talent who dug a hole and buried his talent. This man was full of excuses for why he didn't do anything with the talent.

There are always lots of excuses for why we don't grow, increase, or improve. Someone once said, "Excuses are like armpits. There are usually two of them and they stink." This man in the parable ended up losing his talent to someone else.

The master rebuked this man for being wicked and lazy. He found it inexcusable that the man didn't even make the smallest effort to do something with the talent he was given.

Teenagers need to be challenged to do something with their lives. What can they do right now with the talents given to them by God? They must be challenged academically. Their attitudes toward school and work, and their basic attitudes toward life, need to be challenged. Otherwise, they could end up losing out and becoming totally unprofitable.

It takes a lot of hard work to multiply talents. It also takes a lot of time and effort for teenagers to improve in their academics, but I believe it is possible. In First Corinthians 15:10, Paul explained very clearly what made him a success.

*But by the **grace** of God I am what I am, and His **grace** toward me was not in vain; but I labored more abundantly than they all, yet not I, but the **grace** of God which was with me* (1 Corinthians 15:10).

Here Paul provides two important principles that helped him multiply his talents. First, he said it took a lot of hard work. He labored more abundantly than others. Sometimes others can start slowing down, but you can't let that influence you. God is a rewarder of the diligent (see Heb. 11:6). The way to multiply your talents is comparable to the life of an athlete. You improve only as you invest your time and energy. For example, I love playing tennis. The more I play and the more I practice, the better I get. So in effect, Paul said, "I have chosen to pour all my energies into becoming better at being an apostle." He became a great apostle because he labored hard at it.

Second, Paul depended fully on the grace of God. Three times in one verse, Paul brags on the grace of God, or the supernatural ability of God, that made him what he was.

With Paul's work ethic and total dependence on the grace of God, he surpassed even the other apostles who were before him. Paul was not laboring to be competitive with the other disciples, but to try his very hardest to make his life count for the glory of God.

Believe the Scripture that says, "I can do all things through Christ who strengthens me" (Phil. 4:13). Apply it to every area of your life. Have confidence in the Bible when it says, "Nothing is impossible" (Lk. 1:37).

If young people are challenged the right way, they can become excellent at school and in life, and multiply their talents for the glory of God.

Now let's look at the people in this parable who didn't have a problem with laziness. They were the good, faithful, and industrious people who automatically did something with what the master gave them. Notice that in a short period of time, they had multiplied their talents.

The man with two talents doubled his talent. The man with five talents also doubled his talents. These men did the right thing with their talents and they not only increased and added to their talents, but also actually doubled them. It is exciting when we apply the principles of this parable to every gift and talent we have from God. We can take what God has given us and double the talent through use, wisdom, desire, and hard work.

These two men were commended by the master, "Well done, good and faithful servant" (see Mt. 25:21,23). They were faithful stewards with what was given them, and because they were faithful with the little given them, they received a giant leap in their talent amount. They were promoted to being leader or ruler over many things. So it is possible to multiply your talents, to double them, and then to become a leader!

People who don't feel that they have talent in any area of their lives, including brains, can take the little that they have and multiply it to the extent of even becoming a leader in that area. Again I repeat, people don't have to stay at one talent for the rest of their lives.

Besides doubling their talents, these two faithful men entered into the joy of the Lord. There is joy for the people who do something with their talents—the joy of accomplishment! The joy of the Lord is on faithful, hard-working people. Don't overlook or underestimate the reward of joy. It is not the people who are necessarily the busiest in the Kingdom's work who are the happiest, but the ones who are busy and fruitful.

Not only did they double their talents, but they also ended up getting the talent of the lazy fellow who did nothing with it.

For to everyone who has, more will be given, and he will have abundance (Matthew 25:29a).

Even on top of what they had doubled, they were given more abundance. More is on the way for these types of people.

The parable in Luke 19:11-27 is a little different in that ten servants were all given the same amount—one mina each. Some people could extract from this parable that we have all been given the same amount of talent as human beings. We are all talented—perhaps in different areas—but we all have been given at least one.

This story is very similar to Matthew's parable of the lazy man, but this one also contains some additional points we need to highlight.

All ten servants began with one mina each, but two of the men did something better than just doubling their portions.

And the second came, saying, "Master, your mina has earned five minas" (Luke 19:18).

This man with one mina had multiplied his gift five times. What an increase! The man with two talents in the other parable was commended for merely doubling his talents. This man did even better than that. Just think of the fruit we could have in our lives if we likewise increased every talent we have been given by God. The story doesn't end there, though.

Then came the first, saying, "Master, your mina has earned ***ten*** *minas"* (Luke 19:16).

This man not only doubled his mina, not only got five times more, but he multiplied his mina *ten* times. God gave this man a mina and he took what God gave him and multiplied it tenfold! Why is it, then, that we doubt so severely that a slower teenager cannot take the talent given to him and multiply it tenfold? Young people do not have to stay at one mina for the rest of their lives.

One could read this parable and think that God blessed the man with ten minas more than the others and therefore he had more minas in the end. But it's clear in this story that the man did something with what was given him, and so could everyone else.

I want to challenge every youth worker, parent, teacher, or pastor: You can multiply your talents and your God-given ability to influence the youth of your nation. Not only have you been given talents, but you also have been given something even more valuable—the opportunity to be a catalyst and to influence young lives.

Throw away any excuses you hold for why you are not doubling your youth group or even moving into greater numbers of multiplication.

The parable doesn't end there, however. The man who had taken his one mina and multiplied it to ten minas, received one more mina from the lazy servant, and he then had 11 minas. That's not bad, considering he started with only one mina. But there is still more.

And he said to him, "Well done, good servant; because you were faithful in a very little, have **authority over ten cities***" (Luke 19:17).*

This is hard to believe, but the man with one mina is now in authority over ten cities! How much of a leap is that, mathematically—somewhere in the millions? *He was promoted from a one mina-man to a ruler over ten cities in a short period of time.*

Do not neglect the gift that is in you, which was given to you by prophecy with the laying on of the hands of the eldership. Meditate on these things; give yourself entirely to them, that your progress may be evident to all (1 Timothy 4:14-15).

We have been given many good and perfect gifts from God. We have received gifts and talents at birth and at conversion; we've received the gifts of the Spirit and so much more. We must not neglect these gifts and be lazy, but follow the parable of the talents and multiply them.

This is a challenge to young people as well. No matter how talented or untalented they may appear, if they don't use their talents they'll lose them. Challenge teens in their academics as well as in their talents. It will undoubtedly take a lot of work to change because they have had years to develop their wrong study habits. It takes time to change attitudes and to turn bad habits into good habits of study and discipline. The Bible says that if you hang around with the wise, you'll become wise (see Prov. 13:20).

As for these four young men, God gave them knowledge and skill in all literature and wisdom; and Daniel had understanding in all visions and dreams (Daniel 1:17).

*And **in all matters of wisdom and understanding**... the king...found them **ten times** better than all the magicians and astrologers who were in all his realm* (Daniel 1:20).

As you challenge young people, I believe God will help them and give them supernatural wisdom as they labor and multiply their talents.

Chapter 7

The Dating Challenge

*Then Jehu came out to the servants of his master, and one
said to him, "Is all well? Why did this madman come to
you?" And he said to them, "You know the man and his
babble." And they said, "A lie! Tell us now." So he said,
"Thus and thus he spoke to me, saying, 'Thus says the
Lord: "I have anointed you king over Israel." ' " Then each
man hastened to take his garment and put it under him on
the top of the steps; and they blew trumpets, saying, "Jehu
is king!"* (2 Kings 9:11-13)

Jehu had a decision to make when he came out from
being anointed king of Israel...was he going to tell his friends?
As soon as he came out from the inner chambers, his friends
confronted him about what the young "madman" wanted.
Jehu hesitated for a minute, perhaps wanting to avoid the
question.

Friendships have a great deal of influence in our lives
and on the call of God. In this story, Jehu finally revealed to
his friends what God had told him. It is encouraging that his
friends believed in the anointing session and helped in
proclaiming Jehu as the next king of Israel.

Besides having a strong relationship with Jesus, teens also need to maintain high standards in the friends they choose.

Do not be unequally yoked together with unbelievers. For what fellowship has righteousness with lawlessness? And what communion has light with darkness? (2 Corinthians 6:14)

Among the many challenges we need to give young people, the one of friendship is vital. Jehu was challenged by the Lord and the young prophet to rise up from among his peers.

But exhort one another daily, while it is called "Today," lest any of you be hardened through the deceitfulness of sin (Hebrews 3:13).

This verse clearly states that each one of us, even the strongest, need daily exhortation in living for God. If the strongest pastor needs daily exhortation and encouragement, how much more do teenagers? Youth ministries can't survive with just two good services each week. Teenagers need godly friendships that motivate them to stay away from sin and to live for God with all their hearts. If you have young people motivating each other, it makes your job much easier as Youth Pastor. Realistically, as your numbers grow, it becomes impossible for you to contact every teenager every day, and teens need daily contact and relationship.

Many of the young people who are coming to church and getting saved are from broken homes, one-parent families, and situations which we call dysfunctional. We are living in a relationally-injured society. Today more than ever, young people gather together in gangs for security and comfort. As they join your youth group, they need positive strong friendships.

Teens who hang around the wrong friends need a challenge. Because teenagers often run in packs, they may tend to associate with other negative and carnal teens. During an early morning prayer time, the Lord gave me a picture of a pack of dogs running free and wild. Then I saw one dog all by himself. As the pack ran by him, he ran after them to join up. So do not underestimate the power of the pack, especially in younger teens. With this picture I felt that the Lord was encouraging me to help the young people who were battling with the pull of wrong friendships. It is a very strong force and they need our help.

Our challenge as leaders is to get a majority of young people running for God, and others will then join in with them. These young people need to become a stronger force in the youth group and, as they do, they will become better known in the community.

I believe that many young people have a growing desire to be clean and pure even though they don't yet know the Lord. When young people who are on fire for God witness to them and invite them into their friendships, these youth will come and live for God too.

As iron sharpens iron, so a man sharpens the countenance of his friend (Proverbs 27:17).

He who walks with wise men will be wise, but the companion of fools will be destroyed (Proverbs 13:20).

There is an enormous force behind friendships. Good friendships influence young people to be sharper, better, and wiser. Wrong friendships become their downfall to destruction.

The Challenge of a High Dating Standard

In all my years of being involved in youth ministry, I have discovered that the primary reason young people backslide or turn from God is their dating. The force behind wanting a girlfriend or boyfriend is so strong that it overcomes their desire to live for God. Many still love God, but get entangled and trapped by their desires.

One of the responsibilities we have in youth ministry is to train young people to walk in the Spirit and to die to the lusts of the flesh (see Gal. 5:16).

> *But fornication and all uncleanness or covetousness, let it not even be named among you, as is fitting for saints* (Ephesians 5:3).

> *For this you know, that no fornicator, unclean person, nor covetous man, who is an idolater, has any inheritance in the kingdom of Christ and God* (Ephesians 5:5).

This high standard is the challenge of the Bible for all young people and all youth groups. One of our most effective programs that help us give the challenge of moral purity to young people is called "Free at Last." Its main thrust is having young people ministering to young people, encouraging them to make a vow to the Lord and to their parents, to be morally pure forever. Then we teach them how they can overcome temptation and the tempter with the help of God.

We teach young people to walk in wisdom. Wisdom can be defined as "knowing and doing what is the absolute best in every situation." As young people read the Bible, and specifically Proverbs, they will learn wise tips for every area of life.

Besides teaching young people to walk in the Spirit, to walk in wisdom, to set high standards for their lives, and to make solid vows to God in the personal areas of their lives, we also encourage them to attend schools with high standards. High standards provide extra strength. We have implemented and maintained a very high standard toward dating in our

Christian school. The standard is higher than most I have had the opportunity to witness.

Our Christian school has chosen to maintain the standard of no dating or pairing off until after graduation. We have found this standard to be very effective in preserving the holiness and purity of young people in our school. Our church and youth ministry fully support this high dating standard and we teach and encourage all teenagers to follow that standard as counsel based on biblical principles.

It is a glory to God when young people put Him first in their lives. We believe that teenagers should be focusing on things other than dating. We preach and teach that teens should wait to date. Here are some points that we use in challenging young people to wait to date. It is exciting when a teenager can say the following from their hearts regarding dating.

I Wait to Date...

...Because I am zealously serving God and dating might slow me down.

Youth with purpose are busy for God "redeeming the time, because the days are evil" (Eph. 5:16). Dating at this time in a teen's life could slow him down from his full dedication to the Lord.

...Because I don't want to be like the world.

Don't copy the behavior and customs of this world, but be a new and different person with a fresh newness in all you do and think. Then you will learn from your own experience how His ways will really satisfy you (Romans 12:2 TLB).

Don't let the world around you squeeze you into its own mold... (Romans 12:2 Phillips).

What does the world teach about dating and teen sex? We need to look at the behavior and customs of our world and then refuse to let that system squeeze us into its mold. While the world is encouraging young people to live in immorality and sinful pleasure, we need to teach teens to say "no" to the world and to be conformed to Jesus and the way He would have them think and act.

> *By faith Moses...*[chose] *rather to suffer affliction with the people of God than to enjoy the passing pleasures of sin* (Hebrews 11:24-25).

...Because I am stronger than peer pressure.

Teenagers must get the courage to stand for God and tell their peers what God is saying to them and what He has called them to, no matter what their peers think.

...Because I want to please God.

Teach your young people to stay strong in their decision to wait to date because they want to please God, just as Jesus did.

> *And He who sent Me is with Me. The Father has not left Me alone, for I always do those things that please Him* (John 8:29).

> *So then, those who are in the flesh cannot please God* (Romans 8:8).

...Because I don't need to date to be happy.

Teens can enjoy life and being young without having to have a boyfriend or a girlfriend! Teach them how to have fun in groups without feeling as if they are missing out on something because they aren't dating. Teenagers do not have to date to have fun!

...Because I am seeking God's Kingdom first in my life.

Teach young people that the main focus of their lives is serving God and staying righteous. Young people can trust

God that He will give them the right partner at the right time.

> For after all these things the Gentiles seek. For your heavenly Father knows that you need all these things. But seek first the kingdom of God and His righteousness, and all these things shall be added to you (Matthew 6:32-33).

...Because I want God's will more than anything.

> ...present your bodies a living sacrifice, holy, acceptable to God, which is your reasonable service. ...that you may prove what is that good and acceptable and **perfect** will of God (Romans 12:1-2).

So many young people rush ahead and insist on dating and so get off track of God's best for them. Teach them to wait for God's choice for their lives. His choice will be perfect for them—a perfect ten!

...Because I want to be spiritual, not carnal.

Spiritual youth see other young people dating, falling into carnality, and missing God's best for them.

> For to be carnally minded is death, but to be spiritually minded is life and peace (Romans 8:6).

...Because I have strong personal convictions.

I like that word *conviction*. Young people can have strong moral fiber. They need to possess the strength of character within them that says "no" to whatever could pull them down.

...Because I am already madly in love—with God.

"Set your affection on things above, not on things on the earth" (Col. 3:2 KJV). Young people need to direct all of their affection and desire on the Lord. We are to love God with *all* our hearts.

...Because I am not ready to get married yet.

The main purpose of dating is to seek a life partner. Dating before you're ready is mostly just playing around with your own or someone else's emotions.

...Because I realize dating is very serious.

Dating should be a preparation stage that could lead to marriage. Teens are not at the age in life where they are ready to settle down and find the partner God has destined for them. The boy or girl you date in grade ten most likely will someday be someone else's husband or wife.

...I want to be spiritually prepared before I date.

There is a bombardment of satanic attack on young people today that is trying to force them into something outside of God's will. I have watched many young people start dating and right away sensed the enemy's attack on them. The enemy will try to get young people to go too fast and do things they know are wrong.

Finally, my brethren, be strong in the Lord and in the power of His might (Ephesians 6:10).

...Because people stronger than I am have already fallen.

The Bible gives us many examples of people who were stronger and closer to God than we are, who still fell into sin. I say to youth, "Better youth pastors, better young people than you or I have already fallen." We must wait to date until we are older. We must wait to date until we know we are ready and we have the leading, blessing, and strength of God to venture into dating. What makes us think we can play with fire and not get burned? (See Proverbs 6:27.) There is nothing wrong with a good fear of God.

...Because my school, parents, and church have high Bible standards and I will not rebel.

...the prince of the power of the air, the spirit who now works in the sons of disobedience (Ephesians 2:2).

Satan works *in* the children of disobedience. The Bible says that rebellion is as the sin of witchcraft (see 1 Sam. 15:23). A young person needs a great desire from the heart to want to obey God.

...Because I can wait.

Teach teens not to be driven by lust. A good test as to whether or not someone is in love or lust is to wait. Lust can't wait; love can!

...Because I can build friendships without getting serious.

...Talk to the younger men as you would to much loved brothers. Treat the older women as mothers, and the girls as your sisters, thinking only pure thoughts about them (1 Timothy 5:1-2 TLB).

Conclusion

I believe no one will ever regret, in this life or in the eternity to come, having high standards in dating and morality. Unfortunately, the opposite is so real. Recently, one of our teenagers was witnessing at a Junior High School. As he was telling the young people that no matter what they had done, Jesus loves them, he noticed an 11-year-old girl beginning to cry. He went over to talk to her some more and she told him that she had just found out she was pregnant. She was upset about what had happened and didn't know what she would do or how she would tell her parents. Will she have any regrets?

At the next school he went to, he talked to a 13-year-old boy who had caused three girls to get pregnant. Will these kids have any regrets? Oh, the pain in the eyes of parents as they ask for prayer for their teenager in crisis. These two stories are by no means isolated cases. This has become everyday news.

Daniel, in the Bible, "purposed in his heart that he would not defile himself with the portion of the king's delicacies..." (Dan. 1:8). Not only did Daniel stand strong, but I believe he also was a major influence on his three friends, helping them to take a high standard in their lives too. When being forced with death threats to bow their knees to a false god, Daniel's three friends decided not to bow (see Dan. 3). Many forces are trying to get young people to bow to the pleasures of sin, but these teens can stand with conviction and say, "I will not bow!" If young people wait until temptation comes to set a high standard, it will be too late.

Practical Tips for Young Adults Ready to Date

Dating can be the most exciting time in a young adult's life, but also can end up being one of the most hurtful. Dating is not a joke. Here are some guidelines that I give to the college and career group about dating.

They Should Ask for Input

As young people mature and begin to pursue dating relationships, we encourage them to get the counsel, input, and blessing of their parents and the church pastors over them.

Obey those who rule over you, and be submissive, for they watch out for your souls, as those who must give account. Let them do so with joy and not with grief, for that would be unprofitable for you (Hebrews 13:17).

Pastors have an awesome responsibility. Someday they will stand before God and give an account for the souls that were under their ministry.

We believe in a balance in this area of authority. We know the Bible says that we are not to be lords over God's church, but to be examples (see 1 Pet. 5:3). We are to watch over, teach, and speak the Word of God into them, with a heart of love.

It is imperative that young daters listen to the input given to them from people who care for and love them. Many verses in the Bible refer to ignoring or disregarding counsel as foolishness. So teach young adults to seek out advice in this area, as well as in every other area of their lives. Receiving advice can possibly save them from missing God, getting hurt, and doing things in a way not taught by the Word of God.

We strongly encourage a working relationship between youth ministries and parents. We encourage parents to take the higher standard. If their standard for their teenager is higher or lower than that of the church, it would be good for them to evaluate their standard. If they are convinced that their standard is appropriate and would like to keep it, then they should be careful to do so in a way that doesn't cause a schism in the church body.

If the church has a higher standard, I strongly encourage all parents to flow in harmony with the church for the absolute best for their children. They will not be stunted or miss out on everything if they dedicate their bodies to God in a high form of worship (see Rom. 12:1).

They Should Be Serving God

When daters display zeal and a genuine desire to serve God, they will be spiritually strong and mature enough in the Lord to resist temptations that come against every dating relationship.

Potential daters who seek first the Kingdom of God, will already be serving in the church and have a growing ministry. Young people are ready to date only if they are seeking first the Kingdom of God and not wanting to fulfill their own selfish desires.

I think it is wise for a single to check out how solid a person is before he proceeds and begins to fall in love. There are many sad stories of people falling in love with someone who was just putting on a show of being spiritual. I love being able to give my recommendation to a young girl or guy when she or he inquires about a young man or woman in the church. I am happy to report when a person has a solid relationship with God, is seeking first the Kingdom of God, and is being used by God. Other times I encourage the young person to wait and let the other grow in God a bit more. They don't have to come and ask, but the Bible says it is wise to get counsel (see Prov. 20:18).

They Need Life Direction

It is common sense for people who get involved with serious dating, to already have their life direction set and be well on their way vocationally, emotionally, as well as financially.

They Need to Know the Timing and Will of God

God's timing is so important in dating. The will of God is the most important thing in life.

> ...that you may be filled with the knowledge of His will in all wisdom and spiritual understanding (Colossians 1:9).

We teach teens that 50 years is a long time and since they have one chance at marriage, they had better be ready. They better know God's will.

They Need to Set High Standards

We do not have a collection of "rules," but we teach our youth the high standard of the Word of God. Everything with which we challenge young people in this area, is in the Word of God. One further recommendation we make to the couple is for them to write down what standards they believe the Lord is asking them to follow and then show it to a pastor or someone who will give them oversight and guidance.

They Need Teaching

In your preaching schedule, it is good to plan to systematically preach on such subjects as dating. I address this subject three or four times a year in the college and career group. A good mother decides when the children need carrots and potatoes. Likewise, get your messages from God and study, but also know the needs of the sheep. We are to feed the flock of God (see Acts 20:28 KJV).

Teach them God's high standards and the way to follow righteousness. Teach them about holiness and purity, how to stay clean before the Lord. Teach new converts to give their lives completely to God and to forget dating until they have been a Christian or in the church for at least six months. Such a move is wise, for many young people can come and just be searching for the best-looking date.

Also teach them how to break out of the bondages of the lust of the flesh and the lust of the eyes (see 1 John 2:16). Both young men and women need help and counsel in this area.

Similarly, encourage the young men to be self-controlled (Titus 2:6 NIV).

Dating Is Dangerous

Flee also youthful lusts; but pursue righteousness, faith, love, peace with those who call on the Lord out of a pure heart (2 Timothy 2:22).

I have spoken in many youth groups and it's a sad situation when the youth group is nothing more than a big dating game. Who is dating whom today and who is breaking up with whom? Paul exhorted Timothy to *run from lust* and to *run after righteousness*. Dating is a serious matter and should be done only when it can be understood that way.

Numerous examples in the Bible portray powerful men who also had problems in this area. Some men made very serious mistakes that we can learn from.

David, the greatest worshiper in the Bible, fell morally because of a lack of self-control in relation to the opposite sex. The strongest man in the Bible, Samson, fell. The wisest man in the Bible, Solomon, fell. Unless we are wiser than Solomon, stronger than Samson, or have a heart more after God than David, we should proceed with extreme caution.

Preach strongly to young people. Give them a high standard, an example they can follow, and a high biblical challenge that will save them for exploits.

Double Portion Anointing for Parents

Chapter 8

David and His Father

...Elijah said to Elisha, "Ask! What may I do for you, before I am taken away from you?" Elisha said, "Please let a double portion of your spirit be upon me" (2 Kings 2:9).

We have discussed the importance of Elisha's ministry in Jehu's life. This mighty man from God had a double portion of God's Spirit resting on him, and he had a message sent to Jehu. So in this chapter I want to specifically encourage parents in the ministry they have to their children and teenagers.

It is comforting to see, in this faith-building verse, that it is possible for us to not only pray for God's Spirit to rest on us, but also to ask for a double portion of His Spirit to empower us. As we face the challenge of raising young people today, we need His Spirit resting on us in might and power.

The exciting story of David and Goliath is an excellent model for active youth. We all know of David's great exploits; he killed a lion and a bear, and then went on to become a great hero in his nation by killing Goliath. Every parent would be proud of their child being used mightily by God to affect the nation in which they live.

As we look at some thoughts from this portion of Scripture, I want to remind parents of the potential in their young person to be greatly used by the Lord. Besides talking about David's great accomplishments as a youth of action, we will also look at some keys that helped him become a man of God. The Bible doesn't say too much about David's parents, but I am sure they played a major part in his development.

Right in the middle of the story of David and Goliath in First Samuel 17, there is an interesting verse about David and his father.

Now David was the son of that Ephrathite of Bethlehem Judah, whose name was Jesse... (1 Samuel 17:12).

Five different aspects about David and his father are mentioned here. Why didn't the Bible just call him David? These four extra descriptive terms must be included for a good reason. I love the Bible because, as you get curious and dig a little into the meaning of names and why they are placed where they are, you find a gold mine of information. These phrases give us a glimpse into David and the input his father had.

David's Name

First of all, David's name means "beloved of God, beloved one." It is also from a Hebrew word that means "to boil with zealous love." David was loved by God and was someone madly in love with God. He had devoted love for God. David also was known for having a heart after God's own heart (see Acts 13:22). That is why God chose him to be the next king of Israel. God told Samuel not to look on the outward appearance when choosing the next king because man looks on the outward appearance, but God looks at the heart (see 1 Sam. 16:7).

David's heart was commended by God. A deep love relationship existed between God and David. Youth of action love God from their hearts, and will do great exploits like David did in killing Goliath.

Of course, the name *David* was given by his parents. In the Bible, names are very significant. They are like prophesies given by the parents that set the tone of the destiny that is on their child. I believe David's parents had some indication that the hand of God was upon him from a young child. They were instrumental in setting a foundation in his life for being a zealous lover of God. We, as parents, need to seek God about the plan and purpose He has for the children He blesses us with to raise.

David—Son of an Ephrathite

The next description about David states that he was the son of an Ephrathite. *Ephrathite* means "to bear fruit or to be fruitful." It comes from a Hebrew word that means "to grow and increase and to bear fruit." This implies for us the importance of continuing to grow in God. We are not to be just a nice green plant, but to bear fruit for God.

The Bible says that David's father was an Ephrathite, that he was a fruitful individual. It shows something of his heart for God. He desired to do something great for God and that attitude was instilled into David as well. David, like his father, was someone who had a tremendous desire to do something great for God.

Like a little seed that is placed in the ground and pushes its way up through, so we need to grow in God. How plants grow has always amazed me—the way a little tiny seed can sprout and grow a tender green shoot, then push its way up through even hard ground with a tremendous desire to live and grow.

Once on our holidays, my oldest son Ryan and I were riding up on a mountain chairlift to take a ride down an alpine slide. As we were on our way up the mountain, I spotted a little spruce tree about three feet high. The unique thing was that it was growing out of the rock. Ryan said, "Dad, that tree can't be growing from rock. It looks like rock, but it must be ground." "No, Ryan," I replied, "that is solid mountain rock. That little tree must really want to live."

Successful teenagers need a father who raises them with the right qualities of character. Young people need character to push through obstacles and put the necessary effort into life to become a fruitful individual. That was an important attitude which was transferred to David. When David saw the bear and the lion coming to eat the sheep, he moved in as a well-trained young man.

It is important for all fathers to be like Jesse the Ephrathite. We need to be growing in God and bearing fruit. Many fathers leave the spiritual upbringing of the children to the mother or the youth pastors. But Jesse was a fruitful man of God himself and trained up David his son to be fruitful too.

David Was From Bethlehem

The next phrase used in this verse states that David was from Bethlehem. *Bethlehem* means "The House of Bread," or "Family With Bread."

Jesse, the father of David, was a father who had a house or family with lots of bread. He not only provided natural bread for his family as a hard-working farmer, but also spiritual bread. In the Bible bread is a type or symbol of Jesus as the "Word of God." The Word of God is our "bread of life," and we must have it in our families. So many families are too busy. Many fathers don't do very well at giving their family something from the Word of God or at feeding their children spiritually.

I challenge fathers to feed on the Word of God themselves and to let the Word of God make them a strong "spiritual" father. As you get into the Bible yourself, God will give you living bread to give to your family.

Family devotions are life-giving, but so few families have them. A good place to start is at breakfast or supper, when all the family is present. Read some Bible passages and have each person pray. Each day my family has a list of different things we pray for. So it doesn't have to be boring. On the contrary, it can be interesting.

Make sure every one of your children is reading the Bible every day. If they are young, read them a Bible story before they go to bed. As they get older, there are good Bible storybooks and comic books available for every level of reading skill. Both young men and young women need to be strong in the Word of God.

I have written to you, young men, because you are strong, and the word of God abides in you, and you have overcome the wicked one (1 John 2:14b).

If we want young people to overcome the wicked one and to do other great exploits, we must ensure that they are eating the solid meat and bread from the Word of God!

Bethlehem as the house of bread also speaks of the church, a place where people can come and hear the Word of God preached and grow stronger spiritually. Fathers need to be committed to the local church. Commitment to church attendance and church life is crucial! We fathers must make church a major priority as we seek first the Kingdom of God and His righteousness (see Mt. 6:33). There could be all kinds of excuses to miss church, but I want to challenge every father to never miss it. Even while on holidays, find the nearest powerful church and get there.

I am a strong believer in the local church. Young people need to have a foundational background of being in Bethlehem, a part of the "family with bread." Some churches have a strong youth group, but how many teens come to church on Sunday? We teach our young people that the most important service of the week is Sunday morning. That is the time when they can come and hear the Senior Pastor of the church bring the living Word to feed them.

David Was From the Tribe of Judah

The fourth phrase mentioning David and his father tells us that they were from the tribe of Judah. Most Christians know that *Judah* represents praise, thanksgiving, and worship. It was the tribe of Judah who led the army forth to war.

David's father was a man of praise and worship. Nothing blesses teenagers more than a father who is alive spiritually—a father who doesn't leave everything up to the church or Christian school, but by example, teaches praise and worship to his children.

I enjoy getting out my guitar and gathering all four of my kids around me for a praise time. It is terrific! We sing kids' songs. We sing worship songs. Many times we take turns singing a new song to the Lord, one which we just made up. All of them love singing, especially my five-year-old, Karissa. She sings all day. My youngest son, Brayden, who is three, dances around, stomps his feet, and tries his best to sing some of the words of the songs.

David was from the tribe of Judah and had a very important background in praise and worship. He knew how to praise the Lord and how to minister to the Lord on the harp. The first thing that helped with David's promotion toward the call of God after Samuel spoke over him was not killing Goliath. David was promoted because he could play the harp with great skill (see 1 Sam. 16:14-23).

King Saul, because of the affliction of a distressing spirit, commissioned servants to find a man skilled in music to come and play before him. David had just received a fresh anointing from the prophet Samuel and was called in to refresh Saul and help him feel well.

What I didn't know and what I found after a little deeper study was that *Judah* also means "to celebrate and to use the hand to throw." Praise is an instrument of war, not just a way to worship God. Here Judah is mentioned in the same chapter and just verses before the one where David hurled the stone that brought Goliath's doom. Isn't the Word of God great! David, the lover of God from Judah, which means to hurl and throw.

It is interesting that David's hands also are specifically referred to a number of times in this chapter and in the previous chapter.

> *And so it was, whenever the spirit from God was upon Saul, that David would take a harp and play it with **his hand**. Then Saul would become refreshed and well, and the distressing spirit would depart from him* (1 Samuel 16:23).

David from Judah had anointed hands to play the harp and to operate the slingshot.

Contemporary Music

How can I write a book on youth ministry without even mentioning music? So let me interrupt here with this topic. After all, David can be our hero in this area too. He was a lover of God with all his heart, not a lover of the latest music trends. He loved God and played music to express what was in his heart. He was a fruitful young man with the praises of God in his mouth and the weapon of praise in his hands. Young people who have these qualities survive and continue to remain fervent for God.

Many young people have questions about this band or that band. Many youth pastors ask me about music: "What about rap? What about Christian rock and heavy metal bands?"

As a young man, I was never into rowdy music. For a while I was too condemning of Christian rock because I judged it without researching it. We need to be careful that we do not just try to impose the styles we like on others. One thing that helped me change my attitude was a bizarre verse in Habakkuk 3:1: "A prayer of Habakkuk the prophet, set to wild, enthusiastic, and triumphal music" (AMP). He was a prophet of the Lord, not one just speaking a prophecy. I think it is safe to say that whatever Habakkuk was doing, he was anointed.

All that is sin and clearly against God, we need to unquestionably encourage young people to shun. It is so exciting when young people give their lives to Christ or come back to God and wonder what they should do with all the secular and ungodly music they listened to. I say, "Let's have a bonfire." I might preach on music, then encourage everyone to clean up what music they have that is not pleasing to the Lord and inspire them to bring it for a big, after-service bonfire. We sing and shout around a big fire and then everyone throws in the records, books, and tapes they brought. One young man once brought records worth over a thousand dollars. It was a victory party!

Here are some other things I say to help young people to decide what is best for them and not just what feels or sounds good.

Be Pleasing to God

*And He who sent Me is with Me. The Father has not left Me alone, for **I always do those things that please Him*** (John 8:29).

Be an Example

All young people are called to be an example. In First Timothy 4:12, Paul exhorts Timothy to be an example "in word, in conduct, in love, in spirit, in faith, in purity." Young people need to be encouraged not just to live to themselves, but also to set a good example for the new converts and other people in the church. For instance, could they recommend a certain tape they listen to, to everyone?

Make Sure It Helps You Grow Closer to God

All things are lawful for me, but not all things are helpful; all things are lawful for me, but not all things edify (1 Corinthians 10:23).

I believe that music was intended to build us up and make us stronger for the Lord. This verse states that all things might be lawful for us, but does the music we listen to edify our lives? Does it make us stronger people? Does it encourage us to live for God? Many times I see young people with their walkmans on, or carrying their ghetto blasters with the volume full blast, and they look sad and depressed. Sometimes they look mean or angry. I say to them, "I don't care what tunes you are listening to; they aren't doing a thing for you." The Bible says that we judge things by the fruit they produce (see Mt. 12:33). Romans 14:17 says, "For the kingdom of God is not eating and drinking, but righteousness and peace and joy in the Holy Spirit." What fruit is being produced in their lives? Is it joy? Peace? Righteousness?

All things are lawful for me, but all things are not helpful. All things are lawful for me, but I will not be brought under the power of any (1 Corinthians 6:12).

We all know that music can be very addictive. Some teenagers love their music more than they love God. They will choose their music over obeying their parents. If music is in the right place, though, it will not force us under its power, where we worship it and become a slave to it without even realizing. First Corinthians 6:12 in The Living

Bible says, "I can do anything I want to if Christ has not said no, but some of these things aren't good for me. Even if I am allowed to do them, I'll refuse to if I think they might get such a grip on me that I can't easily stop when I want to." The key is, can you easily stop something when God says stop or when you try to stop? If not, you are in bondage to it.

Be a Worshiper

David was a worshiper. He used music to declare his love for God. So another thing I watch is if the teens are worshiping God. Some young people can get so excited about their favorite band, but do they come to church and worship God with all their hearts?

Young people need to be taught that music is spiritual and is a spiritual force. When David played his music, the Holy Spirit came and demon spirits were repelled. Some music does the opposite; it invites demon spirits and grieves the Holy Spirit.

When David played his music, it wasn't just "noise"; it was anointed. Young people sometimes don't know the difference between music that is or isn't anointed. David played, and the Bible says that Saul was refreshed (see 1 Sam. 16:23). His playing soothed the troubled Saul. The anointing of God was on David's playing.

So then, those who are in the flesh cannot please God (Romans 8:8).

This is another fine line that young people need to be taught about. Some musicians play in a band and use it as a way to show off. Others jump and dance around to music and do it in the flesh. We need to be like David and worship with our bodies, souls, and spirits. In Second Samuel 6:14 it says, "Then David danced before the Lord with all his might; and David was wearing a linen ephod." David was doing more than a little bunny hop; he was aggressively worshiping God in the dance. Michal, his wife, looked down and criticized him for the way she thought he was showing off to all the girls (see 2 Sam. 6:16,20). We must be careful that we don't get in the flesh, but we also must be careful not to criticize what others might be doing in their worship to the Lord.

David—Son of Jesse

David had a tremendous father. Jesse was a father who heard from God and named his son David. He was an example of a father who was fruitful, a man who was a spiritual leader in his home. Jesse was a worshiper from the tribe of Judah, which was a major factor in David's upbringing. But the thing I like best in the Bible that describes David's father is the meaning of his name, *Jesse*.

Jesse's name means "to be current." It means "to survive and remain current or extant." Jesse was current and up-to-date with his relationship with God. He knew what God was saying and doing. He wasn't living in a day gone by. What a superb model that is for all parents! It is crucial for parents to hear what God is saying today—to have a fresh touch of God on their lives and in their homes. It is too easy to be stuck in the rut of a way in which God moved ten or more years ago. Some parents try to enforce on their children legalistic rules that God does not agree with at all.

Parents, strive to be current with the Lord. What is God saying to you today? What is God saying to the church? What is God doing in the world? Train up your teenagers to be disciples of the Holy Ghost, to hear what He is saying and doing. Then they can be on track and up-to-date and fit in with Him.

So many young people can meet God at a summer camp and then not be close to God again until next summer. David got close to God and stayed close to God. He probably couldn't have killed Goliath if he had not sensed the Lord close to him that day, when he unexpectedly met up with the biggest challenge of his life.

As I was studying this aspect of David and Jesse, I couldn't help but think of the importance some people place on staying current with the fashions of the day. One year wide ties are in for men and the next year narrow ties are the thing. Now I believe in dressing nicely. There is nothing wrong with nice clothes and having a variety of clothes, but more important than being "in style" with clothes is to be current and up-to-date with what the Spirit is saying today. God's Spirit is always moving and we can't be set in one certain rut in our Christianity. We must hear what is "in style" and "current" with the Spirit. We need to hear what the Spirit is saying to the church today. We need to hear what He is trying to say to us individually regarding our entire life and walk with Him. Then we need to tailor, shape, and fit our lives in line with that. In order to be current with the Lord, we must know what He is saying. Then we must adapt and shape our lives to what is in style with the Lord.

It is imperative that we walk in the Spirit and stay in step with Him, keeping up-to-date with what God is saying today. David is a model for us of a young man of action, current and up-to-date with the Lord.

As youth ministers and parents, we too need to be current with the Lord as well as in touch with the teen culture, which continually changes. Their culture changes so fast it is frightening. It is very important to stay up-to-date if you want to reach the unsaved young people of today. We must communicate the gospel in a way that is understandable and credible to today's young generation.

David got the glory in chapter 17 of First Samuel for killing Goliath, but the father should get a lot of credit too! Four of the five names or descriptive phrases mentioned relate to David's father, Jesse. Parents have an integral part in rearing up successful, giant-killing, God-loving youth.

Chapter 9

Samson and His Parents

Like arrows in the hand of a warrior, so are the children of one's youth (Psalm 127:4).

God has given these young people into our hands as weapons of war that we are to help train, groom, and develop for the Lord. Fortunately, the Bible provides many illustrations to help parents raise up mighty men and women of God, such as David's father.

Samson and his parents are another example for our instruction (see Judg. 13-14). This story talks about not only the father, but also another key person with a very important role in raising up zealous young people. May I introduce the dynamic mother?

Mothers have such an important task in raising teenagers. I love the story of Samson's mother and how she was used by God to raise up a strong and mighty young man who did great things for God.

It all begins one day when Samson's mother was visited by an angel, and discovered that God had a plan for her. The angel declared to her that she would be barren no longer, but would have a baby. The angel went on to explain that her son would be used by God to deliver Israel out of the hand of the Philistines. So she ran home and excitedly shared the good news with her husband.

Some women feel as if they are just wives—confined, limited, without any important responsibilities in life. I want to blast that concept. Being a mother includes the very great responsibility of raising up dedicated youth. It is a vital ministry that requires the call of God and the anointing of God, just like any other ministry. What a challenge it is to raise young people today, let alone to raise them up to be mighty for God in the midst of a crooked and perverse generation (see Phil. 2:15).

God sent an angel to Samson's mother to speak to her and to give her a message. If you are a mother of a teenager, I want you to be encouraged, because God wants to help you! God wants to speak to you! He wants to give you instructions in raising your active, aggressive teenager. Along with many other great women in the Bible, Mary, the mother of Jesus, did a great job in her important role too.

I remember one day my wife, Connie, had a revelation from God. In our third year of marriage, Connie came to me and said, "Brian, God spoke to me that it is time to have a baby, and that I will be pregnant within two months with a baby girl. We are to call her 'Joy,' because of the joy Jesus has been to us and the joy we have in serving God. We are to dedicate our first child as a joy-giver to others. She will bring joy and happiness to us and many others." It is so exciting whenever you hear from God. Everything God told Connie came to pass. So when a baby girl was born, I of course agreed with her to call her "Joy." Joy really has been a joy to us and to others.

We as parents must be listening to God and seeking God for His plan for the children He has given to us. We have a responsibility to raise them up to fulfill their calling and purpose in God. It's not what we want them to do with their lives that is important, but what God has in store for them.

Like all good husbands, Samson's father, Manoah, believed that his wife met with an angel and heard from God. He didn't want to miss out on anything, so he went to seek the Lord too. He said, "Lord, let this angel come again. Let me talk to him too and hear the message about the son we are to have" (see Judg. 13:8). It is vital for both parents to hear from God about their children. Then they can move in unity to accomplish God's will. So this is a great story of how God used parents to mold their son into the strongest man in history. Samson became someone called by God to do exploits.

We see through this case study that God is calling the entire family into this project. Samson, his father, and his mother all had a part to play in the plan of God.

God also wants to use your entire family for His glory. We see many times in the Bible how God called brothers and sisters into the ministry, and even entire families. Moses had his brother and sister right beside him in the great deliverance from the nation of Egypt and in 40 years of ministry in the wilderness. Half of the 12 disciples were brothers. James, the leader of the church in Jerusalem and writer of the Book of James, was the (half) brother of Jesus. Philip had four dedicated daughters who were used by God in the ministry of prophecy.

It is an enormous task to be in the ministry and to raise your children at the same time. There is a pressure on "preacher's kids" to perform and to be great, exemplary young people. It especially takes a lot of work as parents. I myself have four children. All of them are younger than ten right now and are serving God right along with us, coming to church and being used by God. I am asking God to help me be a good parent, especially as my children merge toward the teen years. I am trusting God to keep them blazing for Him through all of their teen years. There is an attack on all young people, but especially on "PK's."

One reason preacher's kids endure such a strong attack is the high chance that, because the parents are called full-time in the ministry, so will their children. Samson's parents had a big job of raising and training up a young man to be a full-time leader in the Kingdom of God. God spoke to both of them concerning the things they were to do in raising this young man.

The angel indicated that Samson's parents were to have extremely high standards. High standards are very important in raising godly youth.

> *...be careful not to drink wine or similar drink, and not to eat anything unclean. ...no razor shall come upon his head, for the child shall be a Nazirite to God from the womb.... All that I commanded her let her observe* (Judges 13:4-5;14c).

There is no way to stress the importance of getting specialized instructions from the Lord in raising young people. One of the main things God commanded these parents to do was to keep very high standards. God asked them to keep strict standards with Samson. In fact, those standards were probably higher than those of anyone else in their day. That also is the case for Christians today. We must have an elevated standard that is above the world's level—one that is more disciplined than carnal Christianity.

Rigorous standards were given to Manoah and his wife regarding eating and drinking. Youth sold out for God are different than those in the world. They don't take drugs and drink alcohol. They don't let carnal, worldly music get past their ears and into their systems. They have guidelines and standards about what they feed into their systems. Many young people I have seen have higher standards than their parents.

The standards given them were high not only in the areas of eating and drinking, but also in relation to his hair. So listen to the Lord as you pray over standards—even in areas that may seem insignificant. Be sure to follow the Word of God as you lay out guidelines for your teenagers to follow. Remember, Jesus always did those things that pleased His Father (see Jn. 8:29).

Dedicated youth please God with their appearance. Fashion and the recent styles in dress, hair, and other areas of appearance need to be adjusted by the Word of God and His detailed instructions. How does God feel about it? Some parents are so old-fashioned that they want their kids to dress like they do. Other parents are legalistic and do not discern between what is worldly and what is pleasing to the Lord. Parents, you need to get in the Word of God. Get on your knees and find out what is pleasing to the Lord in raising your teens. Talk with your pastor. Make sure you have the Word of God and the Spirit of God behind you as you set principles for your teenagers. If you don't, you could foster rebellion in their hearts. If you set guidelines with the Lord directing you, God will be with you and help you in the molding of your teenagers.

The "Free at Last" program in our church has really helped young people and their families. It is a great tool to help youth make a vow of purity before the Lord. After taking the vow, teens are encouraged to go to their parents and tell them what they have decided to do. We suggest that the parents plan a very special occasion, perhaps take them out for dinner, and present them with a ring or some piece of jewelry they can wear as a token of the commitment they made, to seal the vow.

Samson's parents were blessed with the promised son and they observed God's commandments in raising young Samson.

Judges 13:25 is an exciting verse. "And the Spirit of the Lord began to move upon him...." The Living Bible says, "And the Spirit of the Lord began to excite him whenever he visited the parade grounds of the army of the tribe of Dan...."

As parents are faithful to the Lord in doing their best at raising their teens, the Spirit of God will go to work and start visiting and empowering those youth.

Parents' obedience and faith are important, but only God can start moving on young people. Pray on, parents, that God will visit your teenager. It takes more than loving parents and high standards—God must visit them. Every living person needs a visitation from God and a personal relationship with Him for themselves. So pray as they go to the grounds of the army of God that God will visit them and call them personally; that the Spirit of God will begin to move on them. Nothing is more exciting to me than to see God visiting young people and preparing them for the army of God.

Samson's parents, once barren, were now thrilled to have a baby boy. To top it off, they had a son with a destiny to fulfill and a call of God on his life. The ultimate in joy was to see God starting to visit him. Can you imagine the incredible joy of being involved as a parent in raising zealous youth?

As a youth pastor for many years, it was exciting for me to see young people touched by God and moved upon by the Holy Spirit. But then, with horror, I saw parents pour cold water on that fire and tell the teens not to get too excited about the things of God. Parents must continually seek the mind of God for their teens in order to help direct them into the will of God. In our story, Samson's parents were faced with some new challenges.

As young people grow up, dating becomes an important subject. In Judges 14, Samson noticed a woman and soon became interested in her. Samson's parents were in shock that he was interested in a Philistine girl. " 'Why don't you marry a Jewish girl?' they asked" (Judg. 14:3 TLB). The Bible says in verse 4 that Samson's father and mother didn't realize the Lord was behind the request, for God was setting a trap for the Philistines, who at that time were the rulers of Israel.

Samson's parents heard God speak years earlier about their son, but they didn't have a specific word from God about whom He wanted Samson to marry. I don't want to add speculation, but perhaps if his parents had more understanding about the full call of God on their son's life and what God was directing him into, they would possibly have been a better help in the troubles that lay ahead in Samson's life.

Here is an enthusiastic young man with the mind of God to do something radical and his parents don't understand it. Parents, you need to keep seeking God. God's ways are higher than our ways and His thoughts higher than our thoughts (see Is. 55:9). We must seek God daily in relation to His plans for our youth.

Parents, if your teenager gets a fresh desire for God and wants to do something radical, it is vital for you to know the mind of God for the situation. Then instead of trying to stop them, you can speak added wisdom into it.

In the middle of Samson's story the Bible includes something that is almost hard to understand. God told Samson to go against the Law of Moses and marry outside his tribe and nation—to marry a Philistine. It was part of God's plan to destroy the Philistines. Samson was led by God to do something that was not just ridiculous, but also totally foreign. Shockingly, the Bible says that God was in it (see Judg. 14:4).

We, as parents, need to be sensitive to the leading of the Holy Spirit and not assume that we have figured everything out. God's ways are higher than our ways and His thoughts are higher than our thoughts (see Is. 55:9). We can't be too quick to think we have the full revelation of His will for our children. God Himself will speak to them and lead them to do great things. We need to watch over our family, sort out the things that are fleshly and not from God, and encourage righteousness. Help young people to discern what is right or wrong. Be there to help teach them how to arrive at solid, biblical discernment. Teach them which things are God's ideas and which are not. *It takes radical parents* who have the touch of God to raise up radical young people.

In Judges 14:5-9, the story continues with Samson and his parents going on their way to the city of the Philistines. Even though Samson's parents didn't agree with the wisdom of this decision, they did go with him.

On the way, Samson was attacked by a lion. Satan is like a lion seeking whom he may devour (see 1 Pet. 5:8). It takes much prayer to raise young people today, to give them godly counsel, and to pray them through the attacks of satan. Even implementing all the great formulas is no guarantee that a teenager will turn out okay. I have not yet discovered a simple, three-point plan on how to raise godly teenagers. Prayer and trusting in God's hand to stay on them is our only solid security. I heard of one father who was so concerned that his children follow God all the days of their lives, that he fasted and prayed one day a week for his children to be strong and for God to protect them and be with them. Young people will be attacked and it is the prayers of their parents that can carry them through.

Samson was confronted by the lion, but the Spirit of the Lord came upon him and he tore the lion apart (see Judg. 14:5-6). Praise God! God will help your teens when they are alone and attacked. God's Spirit will come upon them and they will not only kill the lion, but also destroy and tear apart the demonic forces that come against them.

Samson also gave some honey to his parents (see Judg. 14:9). So there are rewards in raising teens. Sometimes they bring home a "sweet report"—an excellent report card or a special trophy from the victories they have won.

Another difficult area for parents to understand is when their son or daughter has a call to the ministry. Some parents try very hard, but they don't quite understand the will of God for their son or daughter in this area. Parents only want the best for their children. But when they look with natural eyes and lean to safety rather than to faith, they can hinder rather than help their child fulfill the call of God. In our church we encourage teens to respect their parents. If they feel God is calling them to do something radical, something their parents might not quite embrace, than they need to try to win their parents' blessing to go ahead with it.

One Sunday afternoon when I was 16 (and ten months old in the Lord), I was studying in my room for my grade 12 class. I was becoming restless with doing schoolwork. Chemistry couldn't match up to the excitement I felt when I studied the Bible. I was feeling the call of God on my life very strongly. I put my pen down and started praying. Then the Lord showed me a vision of a large arrow. This arrow was pointing south, and right away I knew the Lord was talking to me about a Bible college in Calgary, Alberta. I felt God was asking me to quit school and go to Bible college.

A chilling feeling hit me. I wanted to finish my grade 12, but what would my parents say if I told them I suddenly wanted to quit school and go to Bible college? My parents had raised me well. They taught me to get my schooling. Some of my sisters had dropped out of school and I remembered how sad this had made my parents. I didn't want to disappoint them. I wrestled with this over and over in my mind. Was it really God? I kept feeling a strong impression that this was what God wanted me to do. After settling it in my heart that I was going to quit school and go to this Bible college, I then began to think of ways to share this revelation with my parents. What would I say? "Dad, I want to quit school right now, near the end of grade 12, and go to Bible college"? That would not go over too well, I decided. This Bible college had started six weeks earlier. Nothing seemed to compute. How could I ever finish grade 12? Maybe I could convince my parents that I could finish it later. After all, I was only short one subject—Chemistry. My parents, though, would think I was stupid to quit school when I needed only one more subject to get my matriculation. In the small town school there were no other options. If I quit, I would have to come back another year for a full semester.

Then another problem hit me. All my life, my dad had been sowing the idea of my taking over the farm someday. He was getting on in years and my older brother Jim was already well established. Before I was saved, I had promised Dad that I would take over the farm and be a farmer. Now, if I said I wanted to go to Bible college, it would be a further blow. All the while, I felt the call of God getting stronger and stronger. So I decided to give it a try and if God was in it, everything would work out.

"Dad, Mom, can I talk to you for a minute?" I began. "I felt God speak to me that I am to stop school and go to Bible college." Of course, they were very shocked. After discussing it for a while, they recognized that I was serious and in less than a half hour we were in the car on our way to the Bible college that Sunday night.

Now I was shocked! This was a miracle! My parents had blessed me to quit school and to pursue the ministry. Other miracles began to take place. The Bible college allowed me to enroll six weeks into the semester. The next day, I started Bible college. Also, in the bigger city, I later found out, I could take a chemistry class any time of the afternoon or evening. So the next semester I finished my grade 12 while going to Bible college. Praise God!

I thank God for my parents, that they had understanding for what I wanted to do and what I felt God calling me to do. Even though it was different from what they wanted me to do, they supported me.

Parents, seek God about the destiny of your children and move with what the Holy Ghost is saying. Get counsel from your pastor to get more wisdom. You are not the only ones watching out for your child's life. Hebrews 13:17a says, "Obey those who rule over you, and be submissive, for they watch out for your souls, as those who must give account." Pastors have a very important role in watching over the families in the church. They will seek God and give godly counsel on this matter as well.

The Tower and
the Battlefield

Chapter 10

The Tower:
Action Youth Ministries

For which of you, intending to build a tower, does not sit down first and count the cost, whether he has enough to finish it (Luke 14:28).

Or what king, going to make war against another king, does not sit down first and consider whether he is able with ten thousand to meet him who comes against him with twenty thousand? (Luke 14:31)

The concept of the tower and the battlefield was inspired to me by Winkie Pratney in the middle of one of his sermons. Winkie referred to our mission from this portion of Scripture in Luke, how the Christian life is like a tower and a battlefield. Winkie taught us that the Christian church needs to be out on the battlefield winning the war and rescuing hostages from satan's domain. Then we are to erect towers where we can bring back the people who have been freed from satan's captivity. The tower is a type of the local church.

By using that framework I want to discuss how we can win young people today on the battlefield and then bring them back to the tower and train them up as disciples of Christ.

Our purpose as followers of Jesus is to fulfill the Great Commission. We are to boldly go into all the world and preach the gospel to every creature. Not only are we to go, but we also are to make disciples. These two things sum up a great percentage of the exploits God has called us to.

We are not called to simply get people to say the sinner's prayer. We are responsible for making disciples of them, and helping them to become trained soldiers too. The exploits we need to perform are ones that build up the local church.

In the old cowboy movies, the cowboys were out fighting with the Indians, but when the battle was over they came riding back to the fort. Often, they would be chased by Indians when retreating back to the fort. Sometimes they barely made it into the fort before the gates closed.

Church is a necessary place for meeting the needs of young people. It is a place for healing the hurts of life. The youth group is to be a hospital where the power and love of God is present to put people's lives back together again. The teens being won on the battlefield are wounded individuals who need healing, deliverance, and much more. Young people need help with the problems that they are facing. They don't need pat answers; they need to meet the Lord.

Recently as I was praying for a young man, God gave me a picture of a skeleton inside this young man. I asked the Lord what it meant and He told me that with the amount of abuse and hardship this young man had experienced, everything he had inside had literally been stripped away. He was a mess. He was suicidal. But it was wonderful to see the Lord touch and repair his life.

The tower is a place of recovery where we regain strength and get our energy revived. Sometimes soldiers lose the desire to fight. In the tower they can heal up and get a fresh desire to fight again. It is a place where they can build up their courage again. It is a place of food, care, and refreshment.

Make Disciples

God told us to make disciples of the people we win to God. This word *disciple* literally means "to attach oneself to another for the purpose of molding and training." Every church should implement a system for training and discipling new converts.

We have a program called "One to One Discipleship." It is an exciting Bible study for teaching new converts. It consists of seven Bible studies on seven major, foundational truths. We also train our youth workers to meet new young people as they come to church and to share with them this incredible seven-week Bible study.

Once a young man came to me and asked, "Brian, can I have a straight talk with you sometime? I want to know how you live in victory. You always look like you have victory over sin, but I don't want a sermon or pat answers. I want to talk straight with you."

This young man was wanting to know some practical "how-to's" for becoming an overcomer through the blood of Jesus. Young people need to know that they can live in victory, even though they are continually bombarded with strong temptations from the world, the flesh, and the devil.

"Teaching them to observe all things that I have commanded you; and lo, I am with you always, even to the end of the age."Amen (Matthew 28:20).

We are not only to go and win, but also to go and make disciples out of the followers of Jesus. We need to teach them to observe the things that Jesus has commanded. "Teaching them [*how to*] observe all things that I have commanded...." We need to teach them how to overcome, not just that they need to.

As a parent or youth minister, what are some areas that your teenager struggles with? Don't just tell them to change or to get victory—teach them how to.

No matter how exciting your youth services are, no matter how powerful a preacher you are, even if you have the power of God coming out your fingertips—you still need to touch people one-on-one in a systematic way.

The more your youth group grows, the more you will need a team of care workers to help you in the tower of training to counsel and care for the young of the flock.

In the story of the Good Samaritan (see Lk. 10:30-37), the compassionate Samaritan picked up a man from the ditch, bandaged his wounds, poured the oil and wine on them, put the wounded man on the Samaritan's own animal, brought him to an inn, and took care of him. The inn is a type of the church too, like the tower. We need to find the hurt people on the battlefield and bring them to the inn. A very important thing here is that the Samaritan took care of him. We need to have genuine care in our youth groups.

The next day the Good Samaritan left the inn and delegated the responsibility of the man to the innkeeper. The Samaritan told him to "take care of him" (Lk. 10:35). This Samaritan is an excellent example for us. He took care of the wounded man and then put him into the hands of others also competent to care for him. We always need more than one person. Each individual should be enfolded and surrounded by a caring team of people. Training others to care for people is vital to the growth of a youth group.

Tower for Equipping

Inside the tower was most likely the armory, a storage place for all the equipment. So the tower of training, the church, is a place where we come to learn about the weapons of our warfare. We get equipped with the weapons we have been given by God.

And He Himself gave some to be apostles, some prophets, some evangelists, and some pastors and teachers, for the equipping of the saints for the work of ministry, for the edifying of the body of Christ (Ephesians 4:11-12).

The word *equip* means "to completely furnish or to perfect." It comes from a root word that means "repair or adjust." God has chosen the five-fold giftings in the church to help train, adjust, and perfect the saints to help them do the work of the ministry.

We need to equip and train young people for the work of the ministry that God has for them. They need to be equipped and furnished with the Word of God. They need to be taught to handle our sword, the Word of God. Even Jesus called His disciples to Him and taught them before He sent them out (i.e., see Lk. 9:1). Teaching and preparation are vital.

Young people need to be filled with the Holy Ghost, His *dunamis* power to be strong, to do exploits. For myself, receiving the baptism of the Holy Ghost was a powerful experience that revolutionized my life. From that time on, any questions I had about God's existence vanished. I knew there was a God. The power of the Spirit of God came on me. I felt like I was in a reenactment of the Book of Acts when they were not only filled with the Holy Ghost, but also set on fire. From that time on I have burned with a zeal of the Lord and haven't looked back.

In the tower of training we lead people into a fuller experience with God so they know God, get full of God, and go forth to do exploits.

Tower of Training—Bible College and Christian Schools

A major part of Word of Life Centre's training up young people is the blessing of having a Christian school where daily training can take place. For many years, before we had a Christian school, I dreaded the fall when school would start again. All summer we had camp-outs with the young people where we would get them saved and full of God. But as soon as school started again, we lost many of them because they were back with their old friends and the pressures of school, homework, and a busier life. Now there is a greater consistency because a majority of our young people attend our own Christian school. We train them on Sunday and at youth meetings and they go to a godly school for daily training. This is life-training that is imperative in the development of the strongest young people the world has ever seen.

The majority of the training process needs to be focused on the training of the team of youth workers and helpers you have. It is important to pull aside the strong teens and workers you have and conduct training times with them. We ourselves meet weekly to discuss the battle—how things are going, coming events, follow-up of new people, and the care of all teenagers.

> ...*every branch that bears fruit He prunes, that it may bear more fruit* (John 15:2).

As you train your workers you will see things in them that need pruning. God has called leaders to help adjust and perfect the saints so they can do the work of the ministry and edify the Body of Christ. This verse says that every branch gets trimmed. If it is not producing any fruit, it is chopped off. Your workers need a little trimming here and there. It will help them grow and flourish.

Strategy Centers

Towers were also strategy centers. That is where they would come to evaluate the last battle and discuss coming battles. It also was a lookout tower. They would look out at the battlefield from their tower and perhaps get their telescopes out to take a closer look at what was happening.

We need to have the strategy of the Holy Ghost. We can seek God and hear His plan for what He is wanting us to do next. The church is the place to pray and get the mind of God for our group, city, and nation. It is the place to bathe all exploits in prayer. It is the place to move into intercession for young people to get saved.

Youth events, like every event, need "mega" organizing. Youth pastors, take this as an exhortation to become more administration-oriented. One of the greatest areas of weakness I see in most pastors, youth pastors, and youth ministries is administration.

All pastors, no matter what calling or gifting, need to improve and develop this essential element of ministry.

Planning ahead and getting organized can only help you win more souls and increase your group. One thing we constantly fight to do in our church is to plan ahead. Plan out the entire year and then go into detail for the upcoming four months. Take time to seek God for coming events. As you plan ahead you will get more excited about your events and you will build anticipation.

In First Timothy, Paul exhorts leaders to be good managers at home so they can be good managers of the church (see 1 Tim. 3). For the church to run well and grow, good management is a necessity!

Every aspect of every youth service needs to be prayed over to seek the mind of the Spirit for that particular gathering. Planning and practices also are very necessary to a successful service. The music team needs to pray and prepare like the preacher needs to. We can't throw things together with little effort and then expect God to bless it. We need to strive to be led by God and to be excellent in all we do.

Having Powerful Youth Services in the Tower

We need to seek God and have the touch of God on every youth service. Every meeting recorded in the Bible (at least, that I can find), was exciting. There was never a boring, predictable meeting in the Book of Acts. Even prayer meetings in the Bible were powerful.

And when they had prayed, the place where they were assembled together was shaken; and they were all filled with the Holy Spirit, and they spoke the word of God with boldness (Acts 4:31).

That was not a monotonous prayer meeting. They prayed prayers that were powerful. The building literally shook with the power of God.

The first step to having great youth services is to get sick of low-level services. They are not from God. For some reason we think we can stand up and preach a monotone sermon from the Word of God and think we are representing God.

For the word of God is living and powerful, and sharper than any two-edged sword, piercing even to the division of soul and spirit... (Hebrews 4:12).

When Jesus spoke, people were amazed that He spoke with such authority (see Lk. 4:36). Thousands of people followed Him. Even at age 12 He captivated people's attention (see Lk. 2:41-50).

Here's a good question to ask yourself: How would you do if week after week you had to attend your youth meetings and listen to yourself preach?

Acts 2—A Dynamic Youth Service

The happenings on the Day of Pentecost are an excellent model to base the pattern of our youth services on. Check out these points and believe God for a fresh move.

1. Excited Anticipation. There was tremendous anticipation of what would happen. Jesus told them to meet in Jerusalem and wait because *something* was going to happen. "...but tarry in the city of Jerusalem until you are endued with power from on high" (Lk. 24:49). How many young people look forward to church and youth meetings? Do they have anything to look forward to, anything to anticipate?

Can you tell your young people to come to church because something will happen? I love to feel the excitement in the air when people gather expectantly for a service.

2. Power of Prayer. This service had pre-service prayer (see Acts 1:14). Prayer is a key that unlocks the outpouring of God's Spirit in a service. Prayer meetings need to be powerful. Prayer needs to be earnest, fervent, diligent, vigilant, on fire, with zeal, and full of faith. Everyone who participates in the service, from the song leader and musicians to the preachers and leaders need to come prepared by prayer.

3. The Strength of Unity. "...they were all with one accord in one place" (Acts 2:1). Factions in a youth group are always a cause for concern. Cliques compare and criticize each other. We need to discourage cliquishness that divides and we must solve other, similar problems that isolate and offend people. God commands His blessing on unity, not division (see Ps. 133).

4. The Power of the Holy Ghost. "And suddenly there came a sound from heaven, as of a rushing mighty wind, and it filled the whole house..." (Acts 2:2). God wants to come by His Spirit to every service. As you evaluate your youth services, ask yourself, "Was God there at all, or did we have some nice singing?" Be honest! The moving of the Holy Ghost makes a service dynamic. The wind of the Holy Ghost needs to blow; the fire of God needs to fall.

5. All Heard From Heaven. "And suddenly there came a *sound* from heaven...," (Acts 2:2). They heard from Heaven. When we gather, we need to hear God's heart, not man's opinion. We covet the gifts and the manifestations of the Spirit. The Word of God needs to be preached and to come alive. We must hear from Heaven!

6. All Were Filled With the Holy Ghost. "Then there appeared to them divided tongues, as of fire, and one sat upon each of them" (Acts 2:3). Everyone in this great service was filled with the Holy Ghost. There is one baptism of the Spirit, but many fillings in the Book of Acts (i.e. Acts 4:31). We need to get filled with the Spirit and leave every meeting full of God.

7. Everyone Received. "And they were all filled with the Holy Spirit and began to speak with other tongues..." (Acts 2:4). We don't want a service that blesses one or two people. Every one of the 120 people there received from God. I love services where everyone receives and is blessed by God.

8. Radically Changed. Everyone who came to this service was changed. The power of God fell and they were no longer the same. I believe every service has a destiny from God on it. God wants to change us line upon line—in every service. Second Corinthians 3:18 says, "But we all...are being transformed into the same image from glory to glory, just as by the Spirit of the Lord."

9. Totally Unpredictable. Suddenly it happened! This service wasn't routine or ordinary; it was full of surprises. Any good thing can get old and stale. Have you ever had a drink of lukewarm pop that sat out overnight without its lid? That is the way youth groups can get if they lose their fizz—blah!

Spice up the service with variety. Be creative! Change the entire format of the service into something totally different. Once I moved all the chairs around and put them on risers so the room resembled a TV talk show set. I had a panel of guests and I ran around with the microphone all the while, working the service to arrive at something very meaningful. Another time I turned the entire service into a game show, with two teams trying to correctly answer the questions.

I also love doing illustrated sermons. That is a sermon in which music, drama, and acting take place during the preaching. This method is super for young people. It is fast-moving, interesting, and very often hilarious. It is a great way of presenting a sermon that this visually conscious generation might never forget. These sermons are like modern parables that bring biblical principles alive.

10. Manifestation of the Gifts of the Spirit. Not only do people receive the gift of tongues, but there also should be signs, wonders, and manifestations of the Holy Ghost. We believe for and covet the operation of the gifts in every service.

11. Full of Excitement That Spreads. The news was noised abroad. "Now when this was noised abroad, the multitude came together..." (Acts 2:6 KJV). In the middle of the service, the 120 followers burst through the doors and took their experience to the streets. We too don't go to church and then hide from the world. A good youth service equips young people with the power of God to go where they live and make an impact.

If you have a bad meeting, it will be noised abroad. Have an extraordinary service, and then see what happens! When people hear that you are meeting God, that your meetings are dynamic, they will come. Everyone in the city of Jerusalem heard that something was happening and started gathering.

12. Dynamic Worship. "...we hear them speaking in our own tongues the wonderful works of God" (Acts 2:11). These Christians were proclaiming the wonderful deeds and works of God. This reminds me of Ephesians 5:18-19, which talks about not being drunk with wine but being filled with the Spirit, and "speaking to one another in psalms and hymns and spiritual songs, singing and making melody in your heart to the Lord." They were moving in the gifts of the Spirit and speaking not only to men, but also unto the Lord.

These believers were speaking in tongues, but it was wonderful praise to God with the Spirit's help. God seeks for such worship in "spirit and truth" (Jn. 4:24).

13. Ministry to the Unsaved. A good service will always touch the unsaved. No matter how good a service is, something is missing from it if there are no unsaved present. A good service should always have unsaved there; they should be able to come and see the power of God in demonstration. We are not just to preach the gospel; we also are to preach the Word in demonstration of the Spirit and power (see 1 Cor. 2:4). Paul *fully preached* the gospel with mighty signs and wonders, by the power of the Spirit of God (see Rom. 15:19).

14. Dynamic Leadership. Acts 2:14 says that Peter stood up with the 11 disciples and raised his voice to preach. It is time for youth leaders to stand up and boldly declare the Word of God. I wonder if fire was still sitting on each of their heads? (See Acts 2:3.) I challenge every youth worker and pastor to be Mr. or Ms. Fire. When you lead a meeting, when you are on the platform, when you go evangelizing, when you are in prayer, always be full of zeal for the Lord. Then you will raise up zealous youth for sure!

15. Relevant Preaching. Now we come to the point in this dynamic service in Acts that every good service needs—powerful preaching of the Word of God. This is a great model for every youth preacher. Peter's entire sermon was answering questions. He answered three questions and 3,000 people got saved. We can't afford to be discussing irrelevant, dead, and useless topics.

What questions are your young people asking? Find the answers and preach them. Of course, Peter was giving them a word from God that explained what the Spirit was saying and doing, but he did it in a way that answered their questions too. We need to flow with what the Spirit is saying and doing.

Peter's sermon explained what was happening. In all of our services, we give explanation. If someone gives a prophecy, we explain what is happening so the new people not only feel included, but also have their questions answered. Some churches are so afraid of something "out of the ordinary" happening that nothing does. This in Acts 2 was an "extraordinary" service. They were all speaking in tongues, drunk on the new wine.

As a youth pastor, you need to preach on a variety of topics in a variety of styles. You need to give pastoral preaching. You will want to have occasional seasons of systematic preaching to address such key topics as moral purity. Often you need to give inspirational sermons that fire up and exhort the youth group to action. Sometimes you will need to have a "family talk" when you talk straight and bring order into the youth ministry. Address issues. Teach the Word in an expository style.

Training sermons are also very good, or teaching times on such subjects as, "How to move in the gifts of the Spirit." Prophetic sermons are very crucial, since they lay out clearly what God is saying today.

It is important to have guest speakers from time to time. If you feel one of the areas mentioned is a weakness for you, find a person who can come in and give the needed input to keep your youth group strong.

16. Altar Call. In Acts 2, 3,000 souls got saved. An effective altar call climaxes a great service. The Holy Ghost can move, but nothing can surpass the Holy Ghost moving on people to get saved. Then lives can be changed forever. Immediately after the service in Acts 2, people got baptized. They instantly started obeying the things Jesus had commanded.

17. People Came Back Wanting More. (See Acts 2:40-47.) They loved church! Do your people want to come back? In Acts 2, the people not only wanted to come, but they loved it so much that they had church daily. They couldn't wait for next week. When young people really get saved, they need something more. They can't wait until Sunday or until next week. A busy church is excellent because something is happening almost every night—fellowship groups, witnessing, visitation nights, sports, music and drama practice. I am not speaking of busyness for the sake of busyness. Luke 2:52 says, "And Jesus increased in wisdom and stature, and in favor with God and men." This verse presents the need for us to develop in four basic areas of life. A strong youth group provides the means for that development.

Chapter 11

The Battlefield: Zealous Exploits

It happened in the spring of the year, at the time when kings go out to battle, that David sent Joab.... But David remained at Jerusalem (2 Samuel 11:1).

Sometimes young people can get too comfortable in their Christian walk, sitting in the tower of training. They need to be exhorted to go to the battlefield. One day King David stayed back from going to battle and fell into sin. In fact, he not only stayed in the tower, but he went for a walk on the roof one night. "And from the roof he saw a woman bathing, and the woman was very beautiful to behold" (2 Samuel 11:2b). We can't let young people stay in the tower when God wants them on the battlefield. Not only will they miss out on doing exploits, but they also can turn away from God and get involved in sin. It is essential that young people be zealous and motivated to battle.

As an eagle stirs up its nest, hovers over its young, spreading out its wings, taking them up, carrying them on its wings (Deuteronomy 32:11).

We need to stir people into action. The eagle stirs up the nest to make it uncomfortable so the little eaglets will leave the nest and start to fly. Exploits are like flying. We need to help teens get started. We need to stir them up, prod them out of the nest, and help them learn how to fly.

With proper equipping and training we can get young people ready for the battlefield. The battlefield is where we put into practice what we were taught. It is doing the work of the ministry. It is helping people. A warrior attacks and advances to destroy the power of satan. Exploits are standing for righteousness. Exploits influence our world.

Every youth ministry needs to make evangelism a major priority. Leaders need to teach young people how to become a witness for the Lord, how to share their faith. Most people think they must totally and drastically change from no soul winning to street preaching in one day. I, on the other hand, like to break things up into "bite-sized pieces" that people can get excited about. I like to lead people and cause them to grow stronger and stronger (see Job 17:9). People need to grow in Christ and start doing things they never did before. So to help you, the following is a practical evangelism training plan that will help teens grow in boldness for sharing their faith in an easy, step-by-step way, to get them to the battlefield.

1. Pray

Therefore pray the Lord of the harvest to send out laborers into His harvest (Matthew 9:38).

The first thing you should do to start winning the lost is to begin praying. This first step is so easy that any teenager can do it. Simply lead them in prayer for people they know aren't saved.

Get the young people praying for the unsaved. There really is a hell. Christians need a revival in their hearts about hell. We need a compassion for others who don't know the Lord. It starts with praying and hearing God speaking to you. This is the first step to evangelizing. It is through prayer—prophetic prayer, intercessory prayer, warfare prayer, etc.— that your heart and God's heart are imparted into the youth.

2. Go

Go therefore and make disciples of all the nations... (Matthew 28:19).

Before you open your mouth to preach and share the gospel, you must first "go." I like to get people obedient to the first part; they will find out how to share the gospel later. In this way they find out how much fun and how easy it is. Get them to "go" with you. They can "go" out and look from a distance. I like to encourage young people to come with me and see what I do. Then they are not tackling the whole process, failing, and feeling guilty. "Go"; start with that. Going is easy. It is putting one foot in front of the other, leaving the place where you are, and going to another place.

How many young people can put one foot in front of the other and "go"? See how easy it is to start doing the Great Commission? You can lead the young people who will "go" with you and they can pray and look and watch you do it. You can tell them, "You don't need to do anything but go. Go with me and I will do all the talking."

As they see you and other youth workers do it, they will see how easy it is and be able to begin doing it themselves.

3. Look

Do you not say, "There are still four months and then comes the harvest"? Behold, I say to you, lift up your eyes *and **look** at the fields, for they are already white for harvest!* (John 4:35)

Jesus told us to look on the fields. Something happens when we look at the unsaved. Unfortunately sometimes we forget they exist. But God can start to speak to young people as they go with the purpose of looking.

Again, I clarify to them that all I want them to do is come with me and look. "You don't have to say a thing. All you have to do is come and look, look on the fields of unsaved people. You don't have to feel guilty about handing something out or saying anything. In fact, nobody even needs to see you. Just come and look."

I think it's a great idea to take out some of your young people and youth workers. Just go and look at all the students getting out of school and hanging around their different hangouts. Of course that is not all He wants us to do, but it is a start that all people who have eyes can do. It is both easy and fun.

Once I spoke at a youth convention to about 50 young people. I taught them Friday night and Saturday morning on soul winning. This group of people had never even thought of sharing their faith, but they loved God and really wanted to do it. I said to them, "I am going to go out and preach on the streets. All you have to do is come and watch. Jesus said, 'Look on the fields.' Come and see people who need Jesus." The entire group of young people came out. No one wanted to miss what this crazy preacher was about to do. They came and hid behind cars, trucks, and trees. They peeked around corners. Others boldly stood right beside me.

We at Word of Life Centre take out music teams and drama teams into the streets and parks. We encourage everyone to come and, if nothing else, to just look on the fields. Sometimes I fill a car with people and we drive around, praying and asking God to give us boldness and the strategy we need to win people.

This procedure helps teenagers to get their eyes off themselves and to take a look at people from a different point of view. It is incredible how this has been a major key for people to start having the Lord speak to them. Sometimes the only way to have a burden for a drunk is to go where he is at and just look. The Lord can then start filling you with compassion as you see the emptiness and desperate need that people have for God.

As you are looking at the lost, talk to your group. Tell them what is on your heart. Get them thinking, "What is on God's heart?" Tell them that God can fill their hearts with compassion and that His love can be a motivating factor in their beginning to share their faith more.

4. Go With Others

Jesus didn't send the disciples out all by themselves. He sent them out two by two (see Lk. 10:1). As individuals continue to grow in evangelizing, you can team them up with someone else who is experienced at soul winning.

In Acts 2, Peter, who a few days earlier was timid and shy and denied even knowing Christ, stands up to preach in front of thousands!

But Peter, standing up with the eleven, raised his voice and said to them... (Acts 2:14).

Even though Peter became bolder when he was filled with the Holy Ghost, having the 11 disciples stand with him gave him even more boldness. What were they doing? I don't know. Maybe they were praying. Maybe they were saying "Amen," witnessing to the facts that Peter was presenting. Maybe they were saying, "Preach it, Peter!"

Sometimes it is difficult to witness to another when you are by yourself. Oftentimes, like Peter, we don't stand up and share our faith when we are alone. But when you are out with a friend, it is easier to stir each other up, and you become bolder. Peter was not alone; he belonged to a group. When you are with a group of people, you gain confidence. A team mentality is exciting!

Many years ago I invited a young street preacher to come to our church for meetings. I went with him out on the streets and watched as he stood up on a park bench by a school, lifted up his voice, and started preaching in front of about 400 students who were waiting for a bus. It was dynamic! The entire group loved what he was saying. The next day I not only watched, I jumped up on the bench too! I didn't do anything, but I was there. The third day I jumped in, gave my testimony, and invited them out to the special youth meetings we were having. It felt so good to stand up boldly for the Lord. It was something I had wanted to do for a long time, but had never had the courage until I went with him.

5. Get Them in Teams

Another thing you can do to help your young people increase in boldness for evangelism is form different music groups or drama teams. Many teens can't just jump up and start preaching, but they can play their guitars or sing. Others skilled in acting can paint their faces and hide behind a clown outfit. They can be part of a team that acts out a little skit or even a full production in a park. Most people will not recognize anyone dressed up for a skit. It's remarkable what courage some shy people can have when they put on black leather jackets and dark sunglasses for a skit.

6. Keep All Evangelism Joyful

For you shall go out with joy, and be led out with peace; the mountains and the hills shall break forth into singing before you, and all the trees of the field shall clap their hands (Isaiah 55:12).

Something extremely important is missing if depression and drudgery accompany a team that goes out witnessing. I believe for joy every time we go out. Sharing our faith should be exciting.

Those who sow in tears shall reap in joy (Psalm 126:5).

As you go out and actually witness and share the gospel, there is joy. We have joy when we are out evangelizing because we are reaping fruit for eternity.

*He who continually goes forth weeping, bearing seed for sowing, shall **doubtless** come again with **rejoicing**, bringing his sheaves with him* (Psalm 126:6).

The Bible says that we can have joy every time we go out to sow the gospel, that we will reap with joy, and that we will doubtless come back with joy as well. What great promises these are to claim!

If a team comes back feeling depressed, something is wrong. You need to do some major evaluation and make some changes. As you teach joy in evangelism and experience joy, a new mentality will spread, like leaven, through your youth group that people are actually having fun sharing their faith.

In the Bible, the disciples returned with joy even after they were beaten. That is almost inconceivable!

*So they departed from the presence of the council, **rejoicing** that they were counted worthy to suffer shame for His name. And daily in the temple, and in every house, they did not cease teaching and preaching Jesus as the Christ* (Acts 5:41-42).

We refer to this verse in our Bible College as the 5-4-2 verse: Acts 5:42. We go out evangelizing five days for two hours a day: 5-4-2! (Doing things like this helps us to memorize Scripture too!) The point is, we can't let anything slow us down from doing exploits for God and keeping the joy that He gives when we do.

7. Teach People How to Give Their Testimonies

An introduction to a drama, skit, or music production is a great opportunity for a young person to give a quick testimony. People can share how Jesus changed their lives. As the shyer ones watch others give their testimonies, they will see that it is easier than they thought.

People gain boldness as they learn to share their personal testimonies. The personal testimony is the easiest, yet often the most powerful, way to speak in front of people. They don't have to memorize what to say because the easiest things to share are the events that they have experienced.

A person's testimony is a very powerful tool in soul winning.

*And they overcame him by the blood of the Lamb and by the **word of their testimony**, and they did not love their lives to the death* (Revelation 12:11).

When you give your testimony you benefit yourself and rehearse what God has done in your life. As a result, you gain confidence in God and in yourself.

[And I pray] that the participation in and sharing of your faith may produce and promote full recognition and appreciation and understanding and precise knowledge of every good [thing] that is our in...Christ Jesus [and unto His glory] (Philemon 6 AMP).

As you share your testimony and all the good things Jesus has done for you, you are reporting actual events that you have experienced. It is a reality that cannot be argued.

And I pray that as you share your faith with others it will grip their lives too, as they see the wealth of good things in you that come from Christ Jesus (Philemon 6 TLB).

Giving your testimony is one of the most powerful things you can do when sharing with people who argue with you over interpretation of Scripture. People haven't much to fight with against an experience.

For example, our family had its share of problems when I was growing up. One of my sisters, Dian, especially had a hard time and we were all really concerned for her. One day Dian came back home from another town she had moved to. I immediately saw a difference in her. Her face was glowing and she was genuinely happy! She shared with us about an experience she had with Jesus. She said, "Brian, there really is a God and I met Him. He changed my life." I watched her very carefully. Dian was so changed that I went to church with her. Her testimony was the thing that God used to open me up to the reality of the gospel. Dian's testimony had an impact not only on me, but also on my sister Florence and my Mom and Dad. Five of our family members received Christ within a few months. The power of a testimony is the power of a changed life.

Young people need to be encouraged and trained to share their testimonies. They need to be gently encouraged to share a small, short portion of it to begin with. They feel so good after they do it the first time. I love watching people stand up and give a short testimony for the very first time. I can almost see them grow in God.

I love the story of how Jesus raised Lazarus from the dead. The Bible says that many people came from all over to see firsthand what happened to Lazarus. To be raised from the dead was quite a testimony. As people came from all over, *many of them became believers just because of Lazarus' testimony* (see Jn. 12:9-11). His testimony was powerful! As we share our testimonies, many will believe in Jesus too. Lazarus' testimony was a major threat to the chief priests because it demonstrated God's existence. Satan doesn't like us giving our testimonies because he knows how persuasive they are.

Young people have as dynamic a testimony as Lazarus because when they became a Christian, they too were raised from the dead. They were dead in their trespasses and sins and Christ raised them from the dead to live again.

8. Teach Them How to Give Away a Tract

Here's an easy one! Passing out tracts is simple. An empty phone booth is potential territory for a tract. Who can't put one there?

We have many testimonies of people who picked up a tract inviting them to church and who then got saved. One such testimony is of an older couple who picked up a tract someone had put under their windshield wiper. They came out to a healing meeting. The wife's arm was so bad that the doctors could not do anything about it. She was in extreme pain and could hardly lift her arm. She was miraculously healed by the power of God. That couple shared their testimony of the miracle power of God and, that same year, led more than 50 of their family and friends to the Lord. It all started because one shy person left a tract on a windshield. It is the least we can do. The gospel is effective on paper too.

The next step is to train young people to hand the tract to a person. Teach them to smile and politely say something like, "Here, sir, may I give you this? God loves you." Or, as they hand an invitation to someone, they could say, "Come and find out how God can change your life." I am sure they will think of many other lines. Some people don't witness because they don't know what to say. Usually the first sentence is the hardest. If you can help them get started by giving them an introductory remark, many of them take off from there and become better and better.

You also can teach them to mingle around the crowd at an outdoor concert or drama presentation. As others are singing, testifying, and doing drama, they can be giving out tracts to the crowd and starting conversations with some of them.

9. Out of Town Trips

We live in an area where there are many small towns within a 50-mile radius of our church, Word of Life Centre, in Red Deer, Alberta. We capitalize on this rich opportunity to take teams out to these towns for evangelistic outreach. Also, we are associated with many other churches that we regularly visit with music and drama teams.

Young people love doing this. It is adventurous and expectation in God is high. Maybe that is because nobody knows them in these towns.

Whenever I am invited out to do retreats, conferences, or outreaches for other churches, I take a music and drama team with me. These are excellent opportunities for them to come and witness and preach on the streets of other towns. So it is not only a blessing to the church we go to, but also another way of equipping young people in evangelism. We have crisscrossed Western Canada as well as taken mission trips to various countries.

One of our requirements for being part of an outreach team is that everyone must be doing at home what they will be doing on the road. They must be witnessing and sharing their faith at home.

Plan trips months ahead of time. Use the trip as an added incentive for them to grow in their ability to share their faith and be a soul winner. Taking people on trips will get them more motivated. Besides, when they come back they will be more inspired to do things for the Lord. Vision can come into their hearts to do things for the Lord as never before.

10. Creative Evangelism

We need to be full of God, full of the anointing, and led by the Spirit with the strategy and methods necessary to creatively reach this generation with the power of God.

Going from door to door is very scriptural, but if that is all you do, it can become very tedious. There are many other ways to find people who don't know the Lord. Variety makes anything exciting, especially for young people. Many leaders try to get their young people to evangelize, but make it sound boring to them. Young people love being radical and will respond to radical evangelism opportunities. They will love it!

God told us to preach to every creature. So when someone heard that a punk dance was coming to Red Deer, I said, "Why don't we go and try to witness for the Lord? Let's try evangelizing these 'creatures' for the Lord." Excitement rose as soon as it was mentioned.

Arriving a few minutes before the others at the location of this strange event, I noticed all kinds of bizarre people gathering around the small community hall. I was stunned as I watched these kids with wild colors and configurations of hairdos and clothing. Some were dressed totally in black from head to foot while others had every color of clothing somewhere on their bodies. I started to make my way over, but then took another look at this strange breed of young people. I decided to wait for back-up.

When the others came, we encouraged each other, rebuked fear, and prayed for love and boldness to preach the gospel.

For God has not given us a spirit of fear, but of power and of love and of a sound mind (2 Timothy 1:7).

Many people quote this verse, and they stop after saying "a sound mind." Don't stop.

Therefore do not be ashamed of the testimony of our Lord...
(2 Timothy 1:8).

We are to stir up the power of God so we can step forward and share our faith in a powerful way.

There at this dance, we went for it. We walked over and said, "Hi." It turned out to be one of the most exciting witnessing endeavors I had every experienced. These young people were friendly and extremely interested in who we were and what we were talking about. It was like we were weird to them too, so we got along well. They were young people who had been abused and hurt by many things in life. God gave us a compassion and love for them. They acted the way they did just to survive the pressures of being young in this generation. They were open and friendly, and they insisted on taking us into their slam dancing party. They even let us in free. It was quite an experience!

Not only did we obey God, share the gospel, and be changed ourselves, but one of the band members came with us to church. He is saved and still living for God today.

There are so many other radical, fun, and fruitful things that can be done. We also have done a lot of bar witnessing. Of course, not with teenagers; only people who are mature spiritually and of age are allowed to come.

Another exciting thing we do is blitz major events in our city. For example, every year we enter a float in the city parade. More people attend that event than any other. We have our band singing on the back and between 50 to 75 young people pass out more than 10,000 brochures with the gospel message in them. We also have parked this float in different locations around town every night for a week of outdoor street meetings. We obtain permission to park it on various properties around town, such as mall parking lots. The band will sing for hours from the back of the float. Another idea for the float is to get permission to have your own police-escorted parade any time during the year.

Theaters, as you know, are a major youth hangout. On several occasions I have enjoyed blitzing those areas, especially when a controversial movie was being shown. One time we went and passed out free copies of the Gospel of John. Many times we have set up a little battery-powered sound system outside the theater and sing and preach (using a microphone) to the crowds as they come out.

As Jehu changed his nation, so I believe that this young generation can change their nations by pulling down strongholds, declaring war on the enemy, and influencing our world for righteousness.

Chapter 12

The Battlefield: Reaching Schools

Of course, one of the greatest fishing holes for reaching teenagers is at Junior and Senior High Schools. Ever since I was called to work with teens, I have had the faith that I could penetrate schools and touch students for Jesus.

No man shall be able to stand before you all the days of your life; as I was with Moses, so I will be with you. I will not leave you nor forsake you (Joshua 1:5).

This promise that was given to Joshua also gave me the faith that I was called to reach out to schools, and I knew that God would give me the strategy to get into those schools. The strategies were different for each city of Canaan that they overcame. Likewise, we need unique strategies for every individual school we try to get in.

You must have the desire and faith that you can and will get into the schools. God will show you the way. One thing I do is pray for the "spider anointing."

There are four things which are little on the earth, but they are exceedingly wise: the ant...prepare their food in the *summer... the **spider** skillfully grasps with its hands, and it is in kings' palaces* (Proverbs 30:24-25,28).

God commends four little animals here in the Book of Proverbs. Ants are a great little illustration; they are *self-motivated, action-oriented insects*. They hurry around with a purpose, working hard during the summer because winter is coming. We too need to be busy for the Kingdom, redeeming the days.

Spiders, on the other hand, are known for their persistence in going where they want to. They are so persistent that they end up in every home, and even in kings' palaces. I claim this Scripture when I am trying to get into public schools. I pray for the spider anointing. "God, I know there is a way of getting into that harvest field. I am going to be persistent and You are going to open doors."

Music and Drama Teams

One day I was having a school outreach planning meeting for the coming year. As we talked, nothing seemed to fall into place. We felt there was something new God wanted to do in reaching out to schools. God had been sending more and more musically talented young people to our church. We were wanting to take bands and drama teams into the local schools, but we had been in them so much we felt we needed something new. We ended up just committing the concerns to God in prayer, and went on our way.

The next day my Senior Pastor came into my office excitedly. "Brian, let me bounce something off you and see what you think." He went on to tell me about how the Lord had spoken to him in a dream the night before. He said, "Brian, we need to take bands, dramas, and rap into the schools. We will call it 'Free at Last.' "

Thus our new program "Free at Last" was born. "Free at Last" majors on issues like alcohol, drugs, and sexual purity. We can't share the gospel in the schools, but we can share a message that is very strong and challenging on moral issues. We have had tremendous open doors in schools, and it has been very successful.

Now we have a "Free at Last" program in our church on Sunday nights every four to six weeks. The "Free at Last" name is spreading through the city and province and hundreds of young people come out from the school to hear more. When they come, they hear the gospel and are challenged to not only give their lives to Jesus and get saved, but also to make a vow to God to be drug free and morally pure forever. As they see other young people run to the front to make this vow or to renew their vows, they are challenged by positive peer pressure to do the same. Excitement permeates the atmosphere at a "Free at Last" rally and altar call.

In order to keep the vow alive in their hearts we have regular rallies and they wear their piece of jewelry (from the covenant they made with their parents), and they wear "Free at Last" tee shirts. Many of the youth also are involved in the dramas, songs, and evangelism "Free at Last" teams we take out. They are part of a movement with peers who are staying holy, clean, and pure before the Lord.

If you don't have a great drama team, start working on one right now. Become professional enough to get into schools and you will discover it to be very effective. Even if you can't get permission to get into the schools to have assemblies, you might try to get permission to set up a little sound system outside on the lawn in front of the school. On a sunny day, the students will hang around, sit on the grass, and listen.

When we first started doing things like this, we took our battery-operated sound system, played sound tracks, and acted out many of the contemporary Christian songs.

If you can't get permission to be on the lawn on school property, maybe you can find a grassy spot across from school property and do music and drama there. Many times we get permission from someone who owns land near the school to do our dramas and songs there. For instance, once we asked a church across from a school if we could set up on their lawn at the noon hour. They were more than willing. They even offered to let us plug our larger sound system into their facilities so we wouldn't have only our small battery unit.

There are all kinds of ways to reach out to today's young people. It is exciting because these are very easy and fun ways to have your young people do exploits and reach out to the schools.

Teach Young People How to Witness at School

Teach your young people how to stay strong and how to be a positive witness at school. They can be used by God to win a lot of souls. I became a Christian in grade eleven. All I did was tell one person I was a Christian and it spread all over the school in one day.

The morning after I gave my life to Christ, I went to school and told my best friend, "Guess what? Last night I got down beside my bed and prayed and asked Jesus into my life." I didn't get too much further when he started laughing at me and ran into the school hallway to tell all the guys before class. "Hey guys, Brian has turned religious. Come on and see." About 20 of my peers came running in laughing and asking to hear more so they could have a really good laugh. Needless to say, that was a very hard day for me. I just about denied being a Christian, but something came on me and I stood up boldly and told them my testimony.

It is important for a student to become known as a Christian. One day my teacher stepped out of our Industrial Arts class. About 20 of those same young guys came into the drafting room where I was working and asked me to tell them more about what had happened to me. I didn't know very much as a new Christian and I had already given my testimony to them, so I started to recount what I was learning in Wednesday night Bible study on the Book of Revelation. I started telling them about the bottomless pit, the last days, and the massive locusts the size of helicopters that would come out of the ground. They were more than interested; they were awestruck and even becoming fearful.

At other times students would search me out at noon hours, come into my lunch room, and demand another sermon. I would jump up to the front of the room and start explaining things on the blackboard. Many young people gave their lives to Christ that year.

Christian Students or Staff

If you already have staff or students from your church in a school or college, you have a head start at getting into those places. A Christian teacher can offer to be the supervising teacher. A teacher or a student can also invite a pastor to come into a class. One time a student was upset when the teacher was teaching immoral sexual behavior. That student set up a class for me to come in and teach for an hour on Christian morals.

Some of the other successful things we have done over the years is form a club or society. We have done this in both schools and colleges. It is very easy to start if you already have some students or teachers in your church who are in that public school or college. After they start a club, they can get permission to book a classroom for a noon hour or after school. Then they can invite you in to conduct a Bible study on current, exciting topics of interest. In some schools, when you form a club or society, they will even let you have some people from outside the school to be part of the core of the group. Try to find every Christian you can. Conscript every Christian student, teacher, principal, and even custodian and bus driver that you can.

When I was just out of Bible college, I drove a school bus for a year and a half. During the hours between the responsibilities of that job, I worked for God. Bus drivers already have access to the school and to many teachers. It was an exciting year for me. I led many of the students to Jesus and most of them came to church. Once I handed out Christian comics, so the entire busload read them all the way home as I prayed and drove. Another advantage to doing that was all 45 students were quiet that day on the way home.

When I was just starting to evangelize in schools, I had free access to about a hundred Christian movies. They were older movies and I wasn't sure how well they would be received. I went to Junior and Senior High Schools in four small communities and shared my desire to start a Christian club to show Christian movies. With great enthusiasm every principal allowed me to come in at noon hours. They usually gave me the library where kids stayed to eat their lunch for 20 minutes. I had the rooms packed out with kids watching these silly movies. After they were finished eating, many stayed around talking to me about God rather than going out to play sports. The funny thing was they loved coming to see these old movies because they were so antique. It was a humorous time, but many souls were won. Then in each town I started a youth meeting on the night that I reached out to the school. The astonishing thing was, I was on school property winning souls for Jesus.

Getting Special Guests Into Schools

Another major method we use is to get a youth speaker, singer, or band in for special youth meetings. When I secure them, I immediately try to book them into schools. Try for assemblies first, but if that doesn't work, a noon hour is also effective.

One outreach that was very effective was a team we had in from England. The school loved them because they were from another country. They sang, preached, and did drama. We had a week-long crusade with them that was fantastic.

Another time we had a speaker and a musician come in. The musician had previously sung with a famous secular band. It was great. We set up assemblies in various schools for an entire week. That Friday night we had a concert. More than 800 young people came out, and more than 80 of them gave their lives to Christ.

We need to keep reaching out and believing for one and two people to get saved, but God also will quicken "big events" to you where you can reach out and touch hundreds. Many will get saved and your name will spread.

Now when this was noised abroad, the multitude came together... (Acts 2:6 KJV).

People will start saying, "There are a lot of young people in that church. They are a good group of young people, clean and pure." Teens will think, "I should go." Or a parent will think, "I should send my teenager to their youth group."

Bus Ministry

If you have a bus ministry in your church, you could make it known that if young people need a ride to your church, they can call for a free ride. You can advertise this in all the literature you hand out. I like to go evangelizing with our buses. We have the name of the church, Word of Life

Centre, printed in large letters on the bus. So even taking the bus with a team of young people to a school and parking it somewhere visible is effective. Also, be sure to get prior permission from the principal to distribute invitations to the evening presentation. Include the bus departure times and locations.

Sports

Sports are excellent tools for reaching out to teens in schools. At some schools I have built up a trust relationship with the principal to the point that he will let me in at noon hours to play basketball with the students. At another school I asked if I could have the gym after school once a week for any students who wanted to come. I assumed all responsibility. Many young people came out. When you do this, you can offer to buy them a pop afterward so you can share the gospel with them. In situations like these you need to be led by God as to when to start talking about Him. Sometimes it is better to go slowly and let something like that become known and even larger crowds start attending. This type of event builds relationships, and once the teens get to know you, they will get saved or come to a church activity.

At one school the first thing I did to reach out was bring a football. One day, as school was getting out, I threw a football to a young man and yelled, "How about a game of football?" He was very interested and gathered about 20 of his friends.

After playing football for an hour, I stopped the game and said, "Hey, how would you like to come to a Bible study that I am conducting tonight?" Eighteen boys from that crowd came. Every week I would go play football with them and get more to come out. In two weeks I led 25 young people to the Lord. The Bible study averaged 20 people per week. It was exciting!

These ideas (and variations of them) will work in any setting. They work especially if you are new to the town, new in the youth ministry, have a small group, or have done everything you know to get inside the school. This also is one unoffensive way of reaching out to the school.

If you are not able to get permission to do things on school property, then stand on public property and talk to young people after school or at noon hours. You could go to the confectionery-type stores where they hang out. We often blitz the schools with invitations to a special youth rally, concert, or our own powerful weekly youth group.

Booking School Facilities

Holding an activity in a school gymnasium or library is effective because it is familiar territory for the students to come to. Sometimes when you invite them to come to a church building they are apprehensive because they are unfamiliar with it. One time we brought in a famous Christian speaker to a small town and saw more than a thousand people pack out a school gymnasium. Other times you can book the gym for a youth activity and hand out invitations for a gym time with something else following it.

For more than five years in the small town of Olds, I booked the gym on Friday nights for our youth activities. I even got the gym for free. During the movie time at noon hours, I would invite all the young people to come out to a free gym time to play basketball or volleyball, then following that we would have a short youth rally.

Bike Draws

A free bike giveaway is a great drawing card for young people. You can ask to do this on school grounds at noon hours and if you can't, do it off school grounds.

For this event we acquire sponsors to donate mountain bikes. We also have given away free pizza or ghetto blasters. (Always keep in mind the importance of appealing to the youth culture.) When we do a bike draw, we set up a little stand and have banners and bikes to attract attention. Always advertise the name of the store or person that made the donation, as well.

To enter the draw, each person agrees to do a 20-minute Bible study at his choice of time and location. Hundreds of young people want to win a bike. They sign up and we team up their names with our young people and youth workers. One day we went through hundreds of Bible studies and 50 people said the sinner's prayer after their 20-minute salvation Bible study. We then record their names, invite them to come to church, and ask if they would like to take the second lesson.

We also send them a letter inviting them to come to special youth activities. It is very easy to preach the gospel to people who agree to give you their attention for 20 minutes.

Passing Out Tracts and Posters

Every school has bulletin boards. Those are great places to advertise your youth group and coming activities. However each school also has different stipulations. Sometimes you have to find a student who goes to the school to put them up for you. At other schools you can't advertise anything that has a fee to get in, so remove the fee. Others don't want the name of a church advertised, so advertise a "catchy" name of the youth event rather than your church's name. There are ways, if you have the spider anointing.

Schools in Other Countries

I also had the privilege of taking teams to other nations. One thing I enjoy on these trips is visiting their schools. We have always had an outstanding response.

On our trip to England, the young people loved us. They don't get to see Canadians very often, and they loved our accent. The schools were completely open to our team, so seven of us split into two teams so we could cover more schools.

On our trip to the Philippines, we went to many schools. But in one larger city in the Philippines, the organizers hadn't tried to get us into the school. I was very upset. I said, "I am going to go to that school and we are going to get in there before we leave this city." I said to the coordinator, "Are you coming, or should I go by myself?" He said, "Brian, you can't get in. It is a busy time right now for the school, plus they can't let you in on one day's notice." I stated again, "God is going to get us into that school. Are you coming or should I go by myself?"

We walked onto the school property and the principal was able to see us. God immediately gave us favor with that man. He said, "I would love to have you in, but not for two weeks." I replied, "Sir, we leave in two days. We are only available tomorrow morning." He really wanted to have us, so he risked his neck a bit and let us in. The next day we were singing, doing our dramas, and preaching the gospel in front of 5,000 Filipinos. It was a highlight of my life.

That night we had an outdoor healing crusade and the response was incredible. The power of God was there. People were healed, lumps disappeared, and deaf ears were opened.

Pray for the spider anointing. Ask God, in faith, to give you the strategy you need to influence your schools and touch them with the power of God. The answer "no" is only temporary! You can get into your schools and do exploits.

Use Any Bait You Think Teen-Fish Will Bite

We have passed out attractive brochures and energetically invited hundreds of young people to our youth conventions.

We say, "Have we got a party for you! Come to our youth convention and see pyrotechnics, a velcro wall jump, bands, lighting, a laser show, drama, music, and excellent youth speakers." They are shocked that a church is doing something exciting. Of course the greatest attraction is Jesus and so they come and get saved. God called us to be fishers of men. Look for the bait that will help the fish bite.

I believe we are close to seeing entire schools turn to God. As we will see in the next chapter, God can give you supernatural strategies to reach this generation with a mighty move of His Spirit.

Chapter 13

Supernatural Youth Ministry: Uzziah, a Man of Action

Every time I read about a teenager in the Bible, I sit up and take notice. God has given us a book that is full of examples for us today. I want to include a case study of another zealous youth who did great exploits for God.

*Uzziah was **sixteen years old** when he became king, and he reigned fifty-two years in Jerusalem. His mother's name was Jecholiah of Jerusalem* (2 Chronicles 26:3).

This sixteen-year-old was reigning as king! All young people can reign in life through Christ (see Rom. 5:17). One of the main facts about Uzziah is that he did what was right in the sight of the Lord. Most people do what is right in their own eyes, as Israel did in the Book of Judges.

In those days there was no king in Israel; everyone did what was right in his own eyes (Judges 21:25).

We need to teach young people to do not just what they want to do, what is pleasing in their eyes, or even what is pleasing to their parents' eyes, but like Uzziah, to do what is pleasing to the Lord. Sometimes teenagers can fool their parents and youth pastors, but Uzziah did what was right in full view of the Lord.

Uzziah Sought the Lord

Here is something even more stunning. Not only was Uzziah doing what was pleasing to the Lord, he also was seeking God. That's impressive! Young people can be on fire at age 16 and be found seeking the Lord with all their hearts.

He sought God...and as long as he sought the Lord, God made him prosper (2 Chronicles 26:5).

Uzziah was a young man who sought God and prospered under His blessing. What a model he is for every young person. I love it when young people can give big offerings because they are blessed by the Lord. Many times young people come to church with only a quarter or a dollar. I want to see young people financially blessed too. Amen!

That reminds me of the story I heard of the conversation between the 1 dollar bill and the 50 dollar bill. The 1 dollar bill said to the 50 dollar bill, "Well, where have you been in your travels since the last time I saw you?" The 50 dollar bill was enthusiastic. "Oh, I have been all over the world. I have been to Hawaii five times and to Japan, England, and Jamaica. It has been a great time! Where have you been since I last saw you?" The 1 dollar bill sadly replied, "Oh, I have been from youth group...to youth group...to youth group."

That is a sad joke, but it is often true, especially in youth meetings. When God starts touching young people, they will be blessed in such an exciting way that large youth offerings will help finance the last days harvest.

The Importance of Seeking God

Uzziah's story shows how important it is for young people to be seeking God. King Uzziah prospered because he was seeking God. We need to challenge young people to have daily devotions and to attend prayer meetings where they can lay their lives before God and get His blessing on everything they do.

Just as the prayer force behind a local church is vital to its prospering, so the power behind a great youth ministry is prayer. Isn't it magnificent that Uzziah at age 16 was in prayer, touching God not just for himself, but also for his nation!

Uzziah's Exploits

For the rest of this chapter, let me draw your attention to the fantastic feats this young man accomplished with the Lord helping him.

And he went forth and warred against the Philistines, and brake down the wall of Gath...and built cities...among the Philistines (2 Chronicles 26:6 KJV)

This young man didn't just sit around and be happy as king; he went forward. It is important to keep moving forward. Not only did Uzziah move forward, though; he went forth to war.

Young people need to wear the armor of God, and they need to keep going forward and winning all the battles they face.

Some of our greatest youth workers over the years have been the young people themselves. People around Uzziah's age get so dedicated and anointed by God that they start preaching, leading songs, and caring for one another.

All 16-year-olds need to be like Uzziah. In their public school situation, they need to seek God, prosper, go forth, win, and be used by God.

The story of Uzziah holds meaning for me because I was 16 years old when I gave my life to Christ and started living for God. I started witnessing at my school and God started using me. It was *exciting*! I asked God to use me and He sent people to come and talk to me, so I could witness to them. I was known all over my school as "preacher," in a good way. God used me to lead many to Jesus. It was an *excellent* start to my adventures with God.

Uzziah, at age 16, was moving onto Philistine land and building cities on their territory. I like the spunk of this young man. He was daring. That is one thing I like about young people—they want adventure. The more risky it is, the better they like it.

The Bible says that God helped Uzziah against the Philistines and against the Arabians (see 2 Chron. 26:7).

So we may boldly say: "The Lord is my helper; I will not fear. What can man do to me?" (Hebrews 13:6)

This young man moved from victory to victory with the Lord helping him. In fact, his enemies even started bringing him gifts.

...His fame spread as far as the entrance of Egypt, for he became exceedingly strong (2 Chronicles 26:8).

Uzziah's exploits continued as he built towers and then fortified them. He was doing the impossible: building towers in the desert, digging wells in the desert, and moving his livestock out to the desert.

God rewarded Uzziah's close walk with Him with overwhelming success in several areas, including military adventures. He also undertook massive agricultural projects in the desert, foothills, and plains.

On top of all this, Uzziah had a host of fighting men who went out to war in companies. He raised up the army of God again into a well-trained and well-equipped army of his day. He had an army of more than 300,000 men (see 2 Chron. 26:11-13).

Uzziah was a teenager when he became king. We need to believe for the hand of God to come sovereignly on the young men in our youth groups. Many times the young women are the first to rise up. Many churches have more zealous women than men. But young men need to rise up and become youth leaders in our churches even at age 16.

Uzziah, to further his brilliance, prepared weapons and equipped his own army. He gave them slings to cast stones, bows, helmets, and spears. In this way he is a type of leaders in the church who give weapons and tools into the hands of the workers of the church.

All in all, Uzziah was a remarkable young man. The verse I like the most in this story, though, is verse 15.

And he made in Jerusalem engines, invented by cunning men, to be on the towers and upon the bulwarks, to shoot arrows and great stones withal. And his name spread far abroad; for he was marvellously helped, till he was strong (2 Chronicles 26:15 KJV).

This man had cunning men on his side who invented engines. He had people who came up with creative ideas and invented things to help win wars. We too have brilliant people who are blessed by God and whom God speaks to, giving them ideas born of the Holy Ghost. God gives us thoughts and ideas to show us how we can be victorious over the enemy every time and how we can reach out to this generation with the power of God.

I can see Uzziah's men up on the towers, slowly shooting with their slingshots and arrows. Then someone gets the bright idea of engines to speed up their shooting. I don't know what kind of engines or devices they were, but they were phenomenal for his day. I love it!

Like the story of Samson, the ending of Uzziah's story is a sad one. All that he had accomplished went to his head and he ended up a quarantined leper until the day of his death. Therefore, let's remember the good points and all the things we are doing right, but let's also always have a caution in our hearts to stay humble before our God.

If we really seek the Lord like Uzziah did, God will make us and our youth group prosper. Uzziah did what was right in the eyes of the Lord as a young man. What an encouragement that is, that young people in every nation of the world can and will live for God, please Him, and do great exploits for His glory.

God Will Give Supernatural Ideas

Just like He did for Uzziah, God will also give you supernatural ideas and strategies. "...'Not by might nor by power, by My Spirit' says the Lord of hosts" (Zech. 4:6). God will inspire not only you, but He will also give your young people fantastic, Holy Ghost inventions to reach this generation and win the war.

In Noah Webster's 1828 dictionary, the word *inspire* means "to draw in a breath, to inhale air. To breathe into or to infuse by breathing. To infuse or suggest ideas supernaturally, to communicate divine instructions to the mind."

God wants to inspire you with God-thoughts. He will suggest ideas to you supernaturally by His Spirit. We desperately need the Holy Ghost to infuse His strength and His divine ideas into us and show us what we are to do.

God Will Give Supernatural Strength

God will also infuse inner strength into you. He will give you the inspiration you need. He will infuse, suggest, and communicate His divine ideas and instructions to you.

I have strength for all things in Christ Who empowers me [I am ready for anything and equal to anything through Him Who infuses inner strength into me; I am self-sufficient in Christ's sufficiency] (Philippians 4:13 AMP).

This entire chapter of Philippians 4 is loaded with key words of confidence. Paul is building up this church to do great things for God. Note all the times Paul said "I have"; "I can"; and "I am." "I have learned in whatever state I am...I have learned...I can do all things through Christ...Indeed I have all and abound. I am full..." (see Phil. 4:11-13; 18).

You hear people say, "I don't have what it takes. I don't have the money. I don't have the time." But Paul said, "*I have!*"

You hear people say, "I can't. I can't overcome my temptations. I can't do anything right. I can't handle the pressure. I can't cope." But Paul said, "*I can!*"

Other times you can hear people with a low self-image say, "I'm not talented. I'm not smart. I'm not good-looking." But Paul said, "*I am.*" "I am the righteousness of Jesus. I am forgiven. I am ready. I am content."

We need to have a mentality change!

I Haven't	——————	**I Have**
I Can't	——————	**I Can**
I'm Not	——————	**I Am**

I Have; I Can; I Am

Say that over and over. Say it with confidence. Say it over and over, stressing each portion like this: "*I have!* I can, I am." Then stress it this way: "I have, *I can!* I am." Then once more, like this: "I have, I can, *I am!*"

God has placed you where you are, and with His strength you can do all the great exploits of Uzziah. God will give you inspired ideas. He will give you the strength to go in, prophesy, and make the Jehus rise up. You are the one whom God wants to anoint to help raise up zealous youth.

Who, Me? Yes, You!

When Ryan was about four years old, he came running to me singing a little jingle that he heard on television one day. I don't know what it was from, but he sang, "Who stole the cookie from the cookie jar, was it you, Dad?" Then Ryan said, "Dad, you need to say, 'Who, me?' after that part." So he tried it again. "Who stole the cookie from the cookie jar, was it you, Dad?" I got my part right and said, "Who, me?" Ryan thundered back, "*Yes, you!*"

That caught on, and we did that over and over. Then one day in church I was preaching and I shouted out to the youth group, "*You can be used by God!*" I got them to reply as one group, "Who, me?" and point to themselves. Then you know what I did? I resounded back with the answer:

"Yes, you!"

We did that over and over again.

You can win souls—who, me? Yes, you!

You can believe God—who, me? Yes, you!

You can move in the gifts of the Spirit—and so on.

Be encouraged, you parents and youth workers. You are key in training up a new breed of young people!

Who, me? Yes, you!

You are called and commissioned by God!

Who, me? Yes, you!

You are anointed for the job!

Who, me? Yes, you!

You need to be positive, enthusiastic, and convinced that God has called you. Then you can be the one to help build up young people to the point where they really believe that they can do it—they can be youth of action!

Conclusion

Chapter 14

R.U.J. Who?

*I have strength for all things in Christ Who empowers me
[I am ready for anything and equal to anything through Him
Who infuses inner strength into me; I am self-sufficient in
Christ's sufficiency]* (Philippians 4:13 AMP).

Supernatural youth ministry is possible only by the strength
of God's Spirit. There is no other formula or any other plan.
Through the empowering that Jehu received, he could do
anything that God asked him to do—even the dreaded job
of overthrowing Ahab and his sinister wife who had killed
so many innocent people.

*Blessed are the poor in spirit, for theirs is the kingdom of
heaven* (Matthew 5:3).

To be poor means to be unable to make a living, to be
reduced almost to a beggarly situation. Poor people are unable to meet their basic needs and so are forced to depend
on others or on society.

Therefore, to be poor in spirit means that we are totally
dependant on God. Those who are totally dependant on
God will possess the Kingdom of Heaven.

*I am the vine, you are the branches. He who abides in Me, and I in him, bears **much fruit; for without Me you can do nothing** (John 15:5).*

We can't allow the spirit of unbelief to hinder us from doing great things. As we stay close to God, His Spirit, and the Word of God, He will do great things through us.

Through Christ we can have all the strength we need. As Philippians 4:13 suggests, we can be ready for any challenge or equal to every force that comes against us. We can be equal to everything that tries to hinder us from doing exploits, through Christ who infuses inner strength and courage into us.

We need to conquer any strongholds of fear in our lives that stop us from stepping out to do things we have never done before.

Jehu was equipped with the power of God. Courage came into him to do what God was telling him to do. Anything that blocked his accomplishing that assignment, he overthrew. He conquered all the things that were holding him back.

One of the greatest exploits young people can realize is to overcome the strongholds in their own lives. When teens overcome obstacles similar to the ones Jehu faced, and even others such as temptation, bad habits, bondages, or family spirits, then a great victory is won in their lives.

I love Jehu's entire story. It offers me continual encouragement and faith for what I personally need as well as for what I am believing for in working with young people.

We need to be like Elisha, who heard the plan from God and called for a young person to help fulfill it. God wants to use young people in His plan, for they too have a destiny.

Many parents and youth pastors are discouraged by the great forces that seem to be winning against the Church.

Many young people are falling into the pleasures of sin, turning their backs on the Lord, and leaving many churches. We cannot allow impossibility to plague our minds. Instead we need to rise up against the forces and say, "We can do all things through Christ."

We need to be like the young prophet. He had a very important part in the story. He was sent to anoint and raise up the next king, the one who would win one of the greatest victories in Israel's history. Young people want to be involved in the plan of God and to be used by God!

Youth ministry is labor that is not in vain (see 1 Cor. 15:58). We are affecting a new breed of young people who will be totally changed and equipped by the Holy Ghost as Jehu was. Get fresh faith that God will anoint you as you preach and train young people. Don't look at all the obstacles and setbacks. Keep pressing forward, believing for great things to happen to and through your young people.

Then, of course, everyone can be like Jehu. "R.U.J. Who?" (Are you Jehu?) Everyone who reads this book can be inspired by the feats this man accomplished. We all—parents, youth pastors, or teenagers—need to be like him.

God's presence can and will continue to change us into the image of Jesus, from glory to glory (see 2 Cor. 3:18). We can go to God and meet with Him in the inner room with all of our deficiencies and weaknesses and come out empowered.

Conclusion of Jehu's Exploits

For many years the great prophet, Elijah, battled with Ahab and Jezebel. Her empire was so strong that even the great miracle of Elijah's calling down fire from Heaven and slaying the prophets of Baal did not break the stronghold that was in the nation of Israel. In fact, it made Jezebel more furious.

> *And Ahab told Jezebel all that Elijah had done, also how he had executed all the prophets with the sword. Then Jezebel sent a messenger to Elijah, saying, "So let the gods do to me, and more also, if I do not make your life as the life of one of them by tomorrow about this time." And when he saw that, he arose and ran for his life...* (1 Kings 19:1-3).

Jezebel caused the greatest discouragement this man of God ever felt. He was so discouraged that Elijah even prayed that he might die (see 1 Kings 19:4). Forces of darkness were strong against the prophet.

Finally the Lord revealed to Elijah His plan for overthrowing Jezebel. We too need prophetic revelation in order to bring down the strongholds standing against young people today. In First Kings 19:11-18, the Bible gives us the famous portion of Scripture where Elijah hears the voice of God as a whisper, not as an earthquake, fire, or a strong wind. God gave Elijah a revelation that He was choosing one of Ahab's captains to rise up and deal a death blow to Jezebel. His name was Jehu.

Finally that day came. Elijah's follower, Elisha, commissioned one of the sons of the prophets to go anoint Jehu and to prophesy the words from God that Elisha gave him to say. Jehu was the man God would use to strike down the house of Ahab (see 2 Kings 9:7).

It is interesting to observe that Jehu's name in Hebrew is *Yehuw*. The first part means that Jehovah is the self-existent and eternal one. The second part means "to go, to walk, to carry." I interpret that to mean Jehu was God's representative, the one who carried His name and the power of His name. He was an ambassador just as we are called to be (see 2 Cor. 5:20). We are also called by His name and we carry His authority.

Jehu was also the son of Nimshi. *Nimshi* means "to bring out, free, loosen, liberate, pull out, unclasp, release, remove, rescue, disengage, untie, and unbind." From this I gather that God was sending Jehu, equipped with His power, to bring deliverance to the people of God—deliverance from a major stronghold! The demonic stronghold over the nation existed through the leadership of Jezebel. This wicked queen and King Ahab were the roots that needed to be dealt with.

Jezebel was a strong, arrogant queen who had incredible loyalty to her gods. She had a staff of 450 prophets of Baal and 400 prophets for Ashereh. It was God's time to finish her off, and Jehu was God's man. However, because there was a major family spirit that controlled the nation, besides Jezebel, Jehu was sent to destroy every relative and friend of Ahab's and Jezebel's.

Jezebel heard that Jehu was coming to get her (see 2 Kings 9:30). The principalities know when we are coming to get them. The army of God is getting stronger and stronger and will continue to increase in the strength of God. When God is with you, you can defeat anything.

I really believe that God is releasing His power in His Church that will affect your nation and the nations of the world. Demonic principalities and powers have been keeping towns and cities bound in strongholds for too long. It is time for us to believe God to use us not just to grow a youth ministry, but to raise up an army that will affect your town and city and then your nation.

> But you shall receive power when the Holy Spirit has come upon you; and you shall be witnesses to Me in Jerusalem, and in all Judea and Samaria, and to the end of the earth (Acts 1:8).

God used Jehu mightily to dethrone Jezebel. Not only was she thrown down to the ground from the window, but Jehu also rode his chariot over her and left her for the dogs, thus fulfilling the prophecy given by Elijah (see 1 Kings 21:23).

All that remained of Jezebel after the dogs were finished was her skull, her feet, and the palms of her hands. Through the power of Christ we can not only bring down strongholds, but also totally destroy and eradicate them to see a great victory for the Lord.

*And the God of peace will **crush** Satan under your feet shortly* (Romans 16:20a).

*Behold, I give you the **authority to trample** on serpents and scorpions, and over all the power of the enemy, and nothing shall by any means hurt you* (Luke 10:19).

God wants to raise up "Jehus" of today to trample on the enemies of God in the land. Many times I have asked young people to stand on their chairs in a youth meeting. Then we act out the verses just quoted. I ask them to look down at the floor. "That is where your enemy is," I declare. "God has won the victory over your enemy and He's given you the joy of sharing in the spoil of a battle you never fought in." I tell them that God wants to make them victors over all the things they struggle with. We give a shout offering and jump off the chairs onto the floor as if we were actually jumping on the devil's head. We stomp on him for a while and then, sometimes, we get up on the chairs and jump off again.

God wants to shake the nations again through great exploits. He is looking for His army of youth *now*! I believe there are mighty and inexhaustible exploits that you and your young people are on the verge of doing!

Exploits of a New Breed

So many youth groups are only trying to stay alive and maintain a small number. Others say, "It is impossible to have godly youth who want to serve God, who want to pray." Some youth pastors say, "I can't even get my young people to sit and listen to the Bible, let alone get them out evangelizing."

Others have believed the lie that young people need a few years to get rebellion out of their systems. They say, "Let them sow some wild oats, and someday they will come back to God."

I don't believe that lie for one moment! God has a master plan. Don't believe anything but what God says. He gave us many mighty, true stories in the Bible to build our faith for the greatest move of His Spirit in history.

Today there is a fresh call of God to go beyond the great stories of the Bible. God is looking to and fro, searching the earth to find willing, ready, and obedient people. He's choosing them and calling them, and as they respond and begin to seek Him and get to know Him, they will be strong and do exploits! They are destined for "heroic acts or deeds of renown; great or noble achievements." God has a high calling for everyone to do great things through the power of His Spirit.

For young people reading this book, I pray that you will be challenged by the Holy Ghost and become a greater force in the army that God is mustering together in this day and that will achieve great exploits! (See Isaiah 13:4.) This army, I believe, will be comprised of the greatest young people the world has ever seen.

A people come, great and strong, the like of whom has never been; nor will there ever be any such after them, even for many successive generations (Joel 2:2b).

God is looking for champions. God is looking for potential heroes...R.U.J. Who?

To contact Brian Thomson for speaking engagements or to request further ministry materials, please write to:

Word of Life Centre
RR #4 Site #4 Box 50
Red Deer, Alberta, Canada T4N 5E4

Phone: 403-343-6570
Fax: 403-343-8480